Communicating Good News

By
David W. Augsburger

Herald Press, Scottdale, Pennsylvania

Communicating Good News is the pupil book of a study course exploring ways to share the gospel in terms understandable to modern man. A leader's guide by David W. Augsburger is available for use with this book.

COMMUNICATING GOOD NEWS
Copyright © 1972 by Mennonite Publishing House, Scottdale, Pennsylvania 15683, and Faith and Life Press, Newton, Kansas 67114
Printed in the United States.
Second Printing, 1973

Introduction

Caring is a new focus for evangelism. Evangelism-that-cares is emerging as a new priority for Christians of many persuasions. Major emphasis on proclamation and social action are coming together. This is happening while the Jesus revolution is making a profound impact upon youth and the results of a decade of emphasis upon mobilizing the laity are beginning to be seen in congregations.

The Christian movement is again being defined in terms of mission. More and more are seeing its purpose as sharing the good news of God's love with the whole world.

Every Christian is a witness. Some are positive witnesses to Jesus Christ; others fumble and communicate negatively. These study materials have been prepared to help common Christ-followers do a more adequate job of communicating the good news which they have already experienced. For centuries most lay Christians have felt too sinful or too inadequately trained to witness. They have left the telling of the gospel to the clergy who have been getting further and further behind. These materials will meet a timely need.

Communication of the gospel must be personal. It must care more about individuals than about numbers. These chapters encourage witnesses to care for the whole person through word and deed as Christ did. A dominant theme is that "the Jesus word must be shared in the Jesus way. Christ is both our word and our way." The message cannot be separated from the method which communicates it. Notice that the chapters in this book have been skillfully arranged into three pairs of message-method.

David Augsburger has filled this book with images. The

images are fresh. They are images that will help translate the good news into the everyday language of the mechanics shop, the electronics studio, and the souls of American, African, and Japanese people. Sometimes they jar and prick the conscience. Taken seriously they will help us communicate the gospel in nonauthoritarian ways into authentic terms that will be understood by the persons with whom we work and speak.

There is plenty of good news to communicate. God is a good God! He wants all persons to be happy and free. He doesn't want any of our neighbors or acquaintances to be guilty, lonely, or afraid.

God's good news can't be contained in a single word or method. Love, power, justice, forgiveness, and relationship are words of the gospel. Identification, demonstration, and affirmation are words basic to the communicating church. They are the key words of this book and the key concepts that will help us anew in communicating the gospel.

Palmer Becker
Newton, Kan.

Contents

WHAT THE GOSPEL IS

HOW TO COMMUNICATE IT

Chapter One
The Good Word of God's Love . . . . page 7

Chapter Two
Putting the Word into Words . . . . page 29

Chapter Three
The Good News for the Whole Man . . . . page 47

Chapter Four
Giving the Jesus- Word in the Jesus-Way . . page 63

Chapter Five
The Goodness of Life Together . . . . page 83

Chapter Six
Following Jesus Daily in Life . . . . page 99

The
Good Word
Of
God's Love
Is this:

While
We were
Yet
His
Enemies
He
Made us
His friends.

While
We were
Helpless
(utterly ugly,
despicable
disgusting)
He
Gave us
His very best.

While
We were
Sinners
(there's no
lower word
in His vocabulary)
Christ
Died for us.
God's One Son.

He
Stopped
At
Nothing
To let us know.
To let us know Him.

(Romans 5:6-11)

WHAT THE GOSPEL IS

The Good Word of God's Love 1

If
You knew
That you
Were loved,
If
You were sure
That you
Were accepted,
If
You were certain
That God is
For you,
That would be
Good news,
The very best!

We have a good word to give.

A five-letter word for love. The most beautiful word for love.

The word is grace.

It is love that comes through when you are unlovely.

It is acceptance that receives you when you know you are unacceptable.

It is forgiveness that frees you when you've done the unforgivable.

That's the good word. The good word of God's love.

It's a word to know, it's a word that must be known. How the word gets around is the crucial matter to be studied in this course.

WHAT IS THIS WORD?

PREPARE TO MEET THY GOD

JESUS SAVES

AT THE END OF THE ROAD YOU'LL MEET GOD

GOD IS LOVE

YE MUST BE BORN AGAIN

> HEAVEN OR HELL? CHOOSE YOU THIS DAY
>
> EXCEPT YE REPENT YE SHALL ALL LIKEWISE PERISH
>
> IT IS APPOINTED UNTO MEN ONCE TO DIE, AND AFTER THAT THE JUDGMENT
>
> CHRIST DIED FOR U

What is this word — the good word of God's love? During the year 1970, billboards across the city of Minneapolis, Minnesota, gave a two-line word:

> **I LOVE YOU, IS THAT OK?** — Jesus Christ

It was the way Central Lutheran Church chose to say it short and simply to all the people of the city. Is that the gospel? Or should it have contained a warning of judgment, a call to repentance, or a threat of hell?

What is the word you give? Is it only one word? One gospel? Must it be said in only one way? With one call?

If you feel that the answer to these questions should be "yes, obviously yes and only yes," then examine the next three testimonies carefully. There are other worlds, and other experiences of the life-changing love of God that are as real and perhaps more real than ours.

A WESTERN MAN

A Moral Law

I knew better. All the time I knew better, but I didn't care. My parents taught me what was right. My older brother followed it to the letter. But me? I didn't want to be a "me too." I wanted to do it my way.

Self-Condemning Conscience

Was I happy? How do you measure it? I had plenty of kicks, but behind it all there was something, something that wouldn't let me forget that I knew better. I tried to put it out of my mind. Who likes to feel guilty all the time? But that's how it was. Just after my big moments, I'd hate myself.

Continual Self-Judgment

When I was a kid, I wanted to spend a weekend at the beach with my buddies, so I lied to my dad. It took me all weekend to get over it.

The first time I had sex with a girl, it didn't mean anything. She cried. I hated myself. I was mad at everything. I hate feeling wrong.

Guilt

But that's me. Always wrong. And angry about it. And guilty. And always punishing myself.

You say I don't have to carry this guilt around with me all the time? I can get it off my back?

But it's part of me!

I can be forgiven? Feel forgiven? That's what salvation means?

That's what I've really always wanted — even when I wouldn't admit it — to feel really forgiven, to know that God accepts me, to do what's right, to be sure that everything's OK. To know I'm saved.

A Need To Be Forgiven, Accepted

AN AFRICAN MAN

It was never far from me, the fear, I mean. The fear that tracked me at all times. I could feel it, always with me.

Primal Sense of Fear

At times it was the fear that all would go against me, against my family. The fear that my crops would blight, my cattle die, my sons grow ill, my good fortunes fail.

Evil Powers Threaten Life

Or at times there's the fear that my enemies may gain some power over me, by some forces, perhaps they can weave a spell through a secret wisdom, and control my destiny.

My father, my father's father, and his father knew how to appease the spirits, to have power with wind, rain, fertility, and good health. If I walk in their ways, the power will certainly be with me.

Troubled Faith In the Past, Ritual, and Tradition

But always, the fears follow me. What if I cannot do what must be done? What if I do not keep the powers on my side? What if all is lost and I cannot become what I must be?

It is power that I need. The power

**A
Need for
Power to
Free from Fear,
From Weakness**

to be free not just from my fears, but from the spirits I fear, from the forces that have plagued and haunted my fathers in many generations.

If your Jesus is Lord of all the powers, if He is master of all the spirits, if He can give me power to live, to do my living, to become all, then I will follow Him.

AN ORIENTAL MAN

I think I had always been lonely. With a great unexplainable loneliness. Even when I was with friends. The heart, even in a crowd, can be frightfully alone.

**Alienation,
Estrangement,
Nothingness,
Emptiness**

I grew up in a close family. We loved each other, each of us in our own way. But the loneliness was always there, even in the best moments of happiness. And when I was alone again, the darkness of feeling cut off would come back again, closing in on me. "Is this all there is?" I would often ask.

**Longing for
Meaning and
Fulfillment**

As I finished my schooling and began work in my profession, the disappointment of the monotonous routine left me terribly discouraged. Near despair. Life seemed so empty, I felt, as we Japanese often say, that "death is the only peace."

Then I heard that Jesus is God's answer of love to our empty lives. I found that He knew all about me, and the faded emptiness I felt, and yet He loved me.

Jesus Christ is indescribably beautiful to me, I could not escape His attraction. His love drew me out. I chose to follow Him in life. And the darkness within me began to disappear. He burst — yes literally burst into my heart with light and joy.

An Attraction To the Lord Jesus, New Light and Life

WHAT IS THE GOSPEL?

The gospel is a word of forgiveness.
The gospel is a word of power.
The gospel is a word of new life.
The gospel is a word of loving relationship.
And it is more. Many times more.

The facts about God's saving acts are unchanging. They have been "given." They are bound up in the historical events of the God-man Jesus. Men do not rewrite the facts of history, although their understanding and interpretation of their meaning may vary.

Any statement of these facts must contain all four dimensions of the truth. 1. The grace of God. 2. The incarnation of Jesus. 3. The death of God's Son. 4. The resurrection to life eternal.

What do these historical facts mean to us? Stated simply, the meaning which makes the news good is "Christ died to save sinners." From what? From the guilt of sin, from the bondage of fear, and from the loneliness of empty meaninglessness as well. The gospel of our Christ is much greater — broader — more magnificent — more appropriate to every tribe, nation, culture, and person than people have often been willing to believe.

What is this gospel — this "good spiel" as the Anglo-Saxon root translates the Greek word meaning "good news"? Let's examine the biblical statements of its content and meaning.

THE GOSPEL IS POWER

"I am not ashamed of the good news of Christ," Paul wrote. To whom? To the Romans. He, a Roman citizen, writing to Rome about this "way of weak and suffering love, that turns the other cheek to violence, trusting in the strength of a God who died like a common criminal." Paul is not ashamed.

"For it is the power of God unto salvation . . . to the Jew first, and also to the Greek" (Rom. 1:16). The evangel is power — not white power, student power, or flower power, but God power.

Later, in the same letter, Paul described this powerful gospel as " . . . what Christ has wrought through me to win obedience from the Gentiles, by word and deed, by the power of signs and wonders, by the power of the Holy Spirit, so that from Jerusalem and as far round as Illyricum [northwestern point of Greece] I have fully preached the gospel of Christ, thus making it my ambition to preach the gospel, not where Christ has already been named, lest I build on another man's foundation, but as it is written,

" 'They shall see who have never been told of him, and they shall understand who have never heard of him' " (Rom. 15:18-21). (Here Paul is quoting Isaiah 52:15, the introduction to the great servant passage. Read it, beginning at 52:7 through to 53:12.)

That is presenting the gospel in power. It is in perfect obedience to our Lord's final commissioning words.

"All authority in heaven and on earth has been given to

me," said Jesus, "Go therefore and make disciples of all" (Mt. 28:19, 20).

"You shall receive power when the Holy Spirit has come upon you; and you shall be my witnesses" (Acts 1:8). Have you noted that the disciples really wanted more "infallible proofs" (1:3) and more inside information (1:6)? "It is not knowledge that will make the difference," Jesus said (1:7), "but power" (1:8). Not infallible evidence, not invincible information, not awe-inspiring knowledge, but the power of a living experience of the Holy Spirit equips men with good news.

The word for the gospel is power. To the Corinthians, Paul wrote: "My speech and my message were not in plausible words of wisdom, but in demonstration of the Spirit and power, that your faith might not rest in the wisdom of men but in the power of God" (1 Cor. 2:4, 5).

For Paul, that experience of power came in the blinding moment of seeing the face of Christ with unprotected eyes on the Damascus Road. He experienced it again when sight returned to his "Son-burned" retinas and he saw the face of Christ in the loving acceptance of Brother Ananias. Magnificent experiences! But for Paul, the gospel was not the power of his personal experience, but the personal experience of power. There's a great difference there.

The experience of power is participation in the power of God which stands superior to all other powers —natural or supernatural.

To the African who senses "the existence of 'gods,' ancestors, and spirits (which should not necessarily be denied), the gospel of power affirms that Jesus Christ is the all-sufficient Mediator between God and man, and the Victor over all evil powers." [1]

Jesus Christ is Lord of all powers that bind and oppress men. "He has delivered us from the dominion of darkness and transferred us to the kingdom of his beloved Son" (Col. 1:13). "Jesus Christ, who has gone into heaven and is at the right hand of God, with angels, authorities, and powers subject to him" (1 Pet. 3:22).

This is an integral part of the gospel. To examine it in depth, read Colossians 2:8-15. It begins with a declaration of man's emancipation from "the elemental spirits of the universe" by Christ, "head of all rule and authority." Then it gives one of the most comprehensive and concise statements of the facts of God's saving acts in Christ, and through Christ in us, and concludes with the word of total victory. "He disarmed the principalities and powers and made a public example of them, triumphing over them in him."

"Conversion, in this context, is a turning around in order to participate by faith in a new reality which is the true future of the whole creation. It is not, in the first place, either saving one's soul or joining a society. It is these things only secondarily. . . . Biblically understood, conversion means being so turned round that one's face is towards that 'summing up of all things in Christ' which is promised, and of which the resurrection of Jesus is the sign and the first fruit." [2]

If that sounds a bit too sophisticated for a simple gospel, say it this way. "The gospel is the good news that Jesus has all power and all authority. He frees us *from* every fear, every bondage, every evil power. He frees us *to* become all we can be in wholeness of being, in fullness of maturity."

That is good news to the African in tribal solidarity with the spirits of his ancestors, with the forces of nature, and with the powers of evil.

It is equally good news to the addict in bondage to the powers of the fantasy world of narcotics; it is identically good news to the devotee of the occult and magical; it is likewise news of victory to the erotically obsessed, to the sexually compulsive. Jesus is power.

THE GOSPEL IS FORGIVENESS

"Repent, and be baptized every one of you in the name of Jesus Christ for the forgiveness of your sins; and you shall receive the gift of the Holy Spirit" (Acts 2:38).

So Peter concluded his first statement of the gospel. His hearers had seen the evidence of the power — experience, heard the source and the circumstances of its availability to all men, now Peter called them to repent and seek forgiveness.

If we say
We have fellowship
With Him
While we walk
In darkness,
We lie
And do not live
According to the truth.

If we say
We have no sin,
We deceive ourselves,
And the truth
Is not in us.

If we say
We have not sinned,
We make him a liar,
And his Word
Is not in us.

If we walk,
In the light,
As he
Is in the light,
We have fellowship
With one another,
And the blood of Jesus . . .
Cleanses us from all sin.

If we confess our sins,
He is faithful and just,
And will forgive our sins
And cleanse us
From all unrighteousness.

If anyone does sin,
We have an advocate
With the Father,
Jesus Christ the righteous . . .
The expiation for our sins.
(1 Jn. 1:6 — 2:2).

The gospel is the good news that God has already forgiven man in Jesus. A person needs only accept it by giving up his self-justifications, admit his helpless need, respond by forgiving all his brothers, and forgiveness is his.

John spells out the good news of forgiveness:
Paul works it out in careful detail:
All have sinned and fall short of the glory of God.
There is none righteous, no, not one.
Every mouth is stopped, the whole world stands guilty before God.

But we are justified by faith in His blood, and reconciled by the death of His Son. (See Romans 3:10, 19, 23 — 5:1, 9, 10.)

This has been — for fifteen hundred years — the dominant and often the sole statement of the gospel. "Guilt and Grace," to sum it up in two words.

St. Augustine, out of his own inward journey through guilt to grace, codified this one dimensional understanding of the gospel in the year four hundred. The Catholic tradition worked it out in intricate detail (morbid guilt, obsessive self-punishment, compulsive good works to achieve release, legalistic obedience the only means of receiving grace). The reformations of Luther and Calvin were largely a return to Augustine. Both preached a guilt-grace gospel stripped of the overlay of traditional self-effort and faith in man's own abilities.

For Western man — American, English, German, Canadian — the fundamental sense of guilt has tended to make his first question, "How can I be forgiven? How can I be free from my burden of sin and guilt?"

The African may ask, "How can I be free from my fears of the evil powers, my weakness, from my enslavement to all the unknown forces that hinder me from becoming my full, true, free self?" But that is not our first question.

Our primary need has been — classically — forgiveness, self-acceptance, and inner peace.

The guilt may be denied, repressed, and go unrecognized. But still it is there. Even among those who have forgotten what to call it or how to recognize its presence, still it is there.

David Shank, missionary in Belgium under the Mennonite Board of Missions, has provided an almost perfect statement of man's need — guilt — and God's answer — grace — in his account of a witness to a group of men who had little awareness of their true condition, and no sense of the way out. A Belgian associate had assembled a group of a dozen and a half foreign miners — Greek, Spanish, and Yugoslavian workers. He invited Shank, who had had little time for thought, to speak.

"What does one say, how does one 'preach to men who have been conditioned by hardness, bitterness, and the propaganda of leftist revolutionaries'?" Shank asked himself. "Presumably their economic, social, and political biases have closed them off to the gospel, so where does the witness begin?" Stripping off his coat and tie, to better identify, Shank followed the translator into the meeting room. Risking everything on a hunch, he proposed:

"Look, fellows, would you agree to play a game with me? Let me try to tell you about yourselves. If I am wrong, you stop me. But as long as I tell the truth about you, I may go on. Agreed?"

They all nodded their cautious agreement, and leaned back to listen.

"None of you men has ever had a real opportunity to get ahead in life until now, and so for once in your lives you are risking your very existence by going down into these dirty, dusty Belgian mines in order that your children won't have to go through what you've gone through up until now. Is that right?"

"Yes, that's right. Go on."

"So then, you work hard day after day, almost batting your brains out down there in the mine so that your kids won't have to — that's your ideal. And when you get your pay on Saturday you go down to the cafe, drink up a good part of your pay, gamble some of it, spend a part of it foolishly, wasting your time so that when you get home with the rest of your pay to give to your wife, she looks at you and tells you that there's not enough money for the week. Is that right?"

"Yes, that's right. Go on."

"Because of your wife's criticism — which was perfectly in order — you get mad at her and slap her? Right?"

"Right, but how did you know?" (Psychologists say that every time that one accuses someone else aggressively it's basically because of his own guilt. But this chap probably thought that I was understanding him in terms of my own experience at home!)

"After you've slapped your wife, you go off in a corner or somewhere by yourself and become really ashamed of what you've done, and then ask, 'Why did I do it? I didn't really want to do that to someone I love! Why do I do it?' Correct?"

"Yes, that's about the way that it is."

"Then you get to thinking and you realize that your kids aren't any better off than they were before, even though that's what you are working for. You realize that you just are not doing what you knew you had to do. You aren't fulfilling your own law — and then you get mad at yourself. You get really mad at your wife; you get mad at the kids. And after you've really been good and mad, you decide that that's about enough of that, and it's time to stop, take yourself in hand, and you tell yourself, 'This next week, things are going to be different.' So you go back to work, back down in the mine, determined that you're not going to let it go like that again. Right?"

"Yes, that's right."

"Then when you go down in the mine again, you begin to ask yourself, 'Will we come back up again or not?' and then you decide not to think about that too much. But you still think about it a little and you ask yourself, 'In case of gas, or a cave-in, or an explosion, then what do I become? What happens to me when I must die?' And then you recall how you messed things up with the wife and kids, and that you haven't done what you should have. And then you wish you could just talk to someone about this, but you know that you can't because perhaps the others are thinking about the same thing, and no one can give any help anyhow. Is this right or wrong?"

"It's pretty well right!"

"Do you know how I know all this?" I asked.

"No," came the reply. "But that's what we'd like to know. Where did you get to know this about us?"

"I got it out of this Book," was the reply. "It's written right here in the Book."

"What book?"

"It's called the New Testament, in which it tells about God's new plan for man. Do you want me to tell you the rest of what it says?"

"Yes, tell us the rest."

"Well, the New Testament, God's new plan for man, says that at every point of difficulty in the situation which I just described there is an answer. God has an answer to help you reach your ideal (what we might call in other terms a moral value structure). God has an answer to your failure to follow the ideal. God has an answer to the guilt that drives you to do things that later you're ashamed of. God has an answer to the unnamed fear that lies at the bottom of your consciousness. What is God's answer? Let me tell you, because if you had a real answer to these questions it would also help you with your problems of feeding, clothing, housing, educating your children." [3]

What was Shank doing? (1) He was following Paul's analysis of man in Romans, chapters one to seven. (2) He was staking all on the belief that these men carried a burden of guilt — whatever name they might have applied to it matters little. (3) He was bringing them to the realization that they stood — mouth stopped and guilty — before themselves, before God, before each other. (4) Then he gave the word of grace — of God's forgiving freeing love that reaches us right at the point of our defeat and failure.

That's the gospel of forgiveness. At the moment a person admits his failure, his sin, his helplessness, he hears God's word of grace. Forgiving all and giving life again.

THE GOSPEL OF NEW LIFE

To the Oriental, the gospel breaks through like light driving out the lonely darkness, like life triumphing over death.

Light, life, darkness, death, these are Eastern images. The Gospel of John is filled with such parabolic Eastern thought patterns. Wind, fire, water, oil, bread, are a few of the many such symbols. The Gospels were written — as far as we know — in a precise Western language, Greek. But they are replete with the Eastern images and idioms of the Hebrew-Aramaic world. The Eastern thought forms and picture words express the experience of God in ways that communicate uniquely with the Eastern mind. Not in the simple propositional statements we know and understand best, but in the experiential images that come nearer to the reality beyond words which Westerners often miss.

Examine only the imagery of John 3. "A birth to new life," "the wind of the spirit," "light has entered the world but men love darkness and hate light," and it concludes with the marvelous statement: "He who believes in the Son has eternal life; he who does not obey the Son shall not see life, but the wrath of God rests upon him" (Jn. 3:36).

To the Oriental, experiencing the darkness of lonely estrangement, Jesus comes like light. To the man enduring the walking death of empty meaninglessness and alienation, the breakthrough to life in Jesus comes like a resurrection.

To the Japanese man, for example, with no word for guilt in his vocabulary (the nearest Japanese translation available is "shame" but that is hardly what is meant by guilt before God and man), it is not forgiveness he hungers for most, but the fullness of life he sees in Jesus, the new life he finds offered to him in the good news of God's relationship with us through Jesus.

It is a gospel of new life, life that breaks into the open heart like light igniting in darkness.

Marvin Yoder, missionary in Hokkaido, Japan, tells of this dawn experience of the gospel.

A widow, a lifelong devout Buddhist, confided in him a great secret she had concealed for years — a secret that troubled her night and day. Her husband, a Christian during the final years of his life, lay dying. As she sat by his tatami, grieving as his life ebbed out, slowly he reached out to her in a gesture of invitation. "Come to me," he whispered.

She knew the meaning of his words. It was his dying wish that his wife die, not as a Buddhist, but as a Christian.

"But how can I curse Buddha and turn to follow Jesus, Yoder Sensei?" she asked. "Buddha has been kind to me through all the years of my life. As a wife, a mother, and now a widow, I have depended on him constantly. Must I curse him?"

"No, you need not curse Buddha to turn to Jesus," Yoder replied. "Jesus asks you only to listen to His words by reading the gospel. If He invites you to follow Him, then you may say farewell to Buddha and come to follow Jesus."

"I will read the gospels," she promised. A few days later she returned.

"A strange thing happened last night," she said. "Tell me if it was real. I had been reading the Gospel of John, and I found Jesus drew me in such a powerful way. It was in the early morning — I do not know if I was awake or asleep. Suddenly Buddha was before me. His face showed a great sadness.

"All these years I have served you well. And now you are about to curse me and go to follow this Jesus?"

"I do not curse you," I told him, "I am thankful for all you have done for me. But Jesus draws me, He promises to lead me where you have never told me I can go. He offers me strength beyond anything I have known. He speaks of life unending."

"As I spoke, it seemed that Buddha turned away and was gone. I was alone. Then I saw the light. It approached me until the radiance washed over me, and through me. And I knew it was the light I had read of in John's Gospel. Jesus was the light. And I heard Him say, 'Do not fear, daughter, come follow Me, I give you life.'

"Tell me, Yoder Sensei," she asked again in conclusion, "was this real?"

"What would you have answered her?" Marvin Yoder asks. Then he adds, "I answered simply, 'It was the most real moment of your life.' "

This is the gospel of new life.

THE GOSPEL OF LOVING RELATIONSHIP

What then is the gospel of Christ? Is it a gospel of forgiveness, of power to free, of new wholeness of life? What of the four propositions Christians have often used to summarize it?

The gospel is the good word of God's love that frees us to live in new relationships.

It is the experienced love of God that meets man where and when he comes to an awareness of his need.

Jesus clears it up in John 17 when in talking to His

Father He says, "And this is eternal life, that they know thee the only true God, and Jesus Christ whom thou hast sent."

Knowing — in the Eastern, Hebrew, biblical sense — is not knowing about, it is not information or data. It is knowledge of. It is relationship. As I write this, my two little daughters are coming downstairs to say "goodnight." There, they're going back up to bed now. A moment ago we had our arms around each other, exchanging kisses on all six cheeks. They did the nightly ritual of finding an unprickly spot on my face to kiss. We delight in each other. We appreciate one another. We know each other intimately. We are more alive when together, because of our love.

That's how we "know" the Father. It is an intimate friendship that gives us rights to one another. The gospel of God's loving relationship is an invitation to friendship.

When a man discovers that God — in love — has been making friendly advances to him, he must either accept or reject that love.

"I love you, is that OK?" God has been saying.

If, however, a man responds by praying:

Father, You want to be my friend?

Then Father, I want to be Yours.

I'm sorry I've ignored You, offended You, even fought You.

I need Your love, Your friendship, Your help.

Please accept me, as Your Word says You will.

Here I am, nothing held back. I'm openly, lovingly Yours.

The Father, hearing this response of loving friendship, and the Lord Jesus, whose terrible death on the cross shows how far His love will go to forgive us, speak out as one, "Of course We accept you. You're adopted — brother, son!"

That's relationship — the experienced love of God.

That's the good news. Say it in the language of every

people, nation, and tongue. Begin from any point, any custom, any need, any experience. This good news is still news too good to be true. Explain it in the insights or the perspectives of every tribe, say it in Heinz with 57 variations and varieties. Relationship is translatable.

It is not a matter of four doctrinal propositions said in perfect orthodoxy. It's a matter of two people in right relationship, and the name of that relationship is love.

Relationally speaking, the good news is God saying to man in Jesus Christ: "I love you. I love you as you are. I love you unconditionally. I've already shown it undeniably by giving Myself totally at Calvary. If you hear Me, show it by loving unconditionally in return, that means give Me all of yourself you can give."

That is the good word, the good word of God's love.

For Discussion

1. If you were asked to put the gospel in ten words or less, what would you say? Do you think all Christians should agree on the same ten words?
2. Is there only one gospel? Or is it like Heinz, provided in 57 varieties, but all with the same name, provided by the same Son, energized by the same Holy Spirit, and bringing the same gift of eternal life?
3. Is it possible that the good news is primarily relational and secondarily doctrinal? Is it true that our doctrine is dependent upon our experience or vice versa?
4. Myron Augsburger suggests, "What we experience determines what we believe; what we believe determines how we behave; how we behave determines the quality of community which we experience." Is this the way the good news reaches us?

For Assignment

1. Write out your understanding of the good news (twenty-five word limit) as you experienced it yourself (not as told you but as experienced).
2. Ask four Christian friends and four non-Christian friends "what (if any) good news does the church have for the world? What, would you say, is "the gospel"? (Perhaps you should assure your not-yet-Christian friends that this is not a trick question designed for you to get hold of their arm and twist.)
3. Ask a no-longer Christian or a non-Christian what was really "bad news" to him in the church and in the gospel as he knows it? (And really hear him without becoming defensive. Don't set him straight!)
4. This activity should be done in class. Draw pictures symbolizing three experiences that have helped you to understand the good news. Using the drawings tell your experiences to another person and have him do the same to you. Now, in a group of four recount your partner's experience. Your partner will check as to how well you have communicated and vice versa.

In
The
Beginning
Was the
Word
(at the
very first,
God
expressed
Himself),
And the
Word
Was with
God,
And the
Word
Was
God
(that
Personal
Expression,
That Word
Was with God,
And was God.)
And the Word
Became
Flesh
(a human being),
And dwelt among us
[And we saw His splendor,
Splendor as of a Father's only Son.],
Full of
   Grace
     and
        Truth.

HOW TO COMMUNICATE IT

Putting the Word into Words

2

*I
Know
You think
You understand
What you thought I said,
But
I'm not sure
You are aware
That what you heard
Is not
What
I meant.*

A Word has been given us.

A Word that is greater than any words ever used to express it.

A Word which must be expressed even though the best words that we may find are insufficient; even though the most carefully chosen words are inadequate; even though they must constantly be changed — or exchanged — for more appropriate words (appropriate to the hearer's understanding), or more complete words (that more completely and faithfully express the truth of the original message given us).

"But what's wrong with the words we've always used?" we are often asked. "Why change the way we say it? Why not just keep on saying it in the same way it was said to us?"

What's wrong with parroting the same words in the same way? It is not words I must communicate, but the living Word of God's love for all in Jesus. If my words become walls, instead of windows, He cannot shine through. And words are so foggy. They cloud so quickly. I must constantly find new words, more transparent words. Words that are more clear, so that He can be seen and heard in my words.

If my task is to talk only to myself, then no change is necessary. Or if I talk only to my own kind of people who share my points of view, who have lived with identical experiences, who get the same meanings out of my words that I put into them, then repeating may be appropriate.

But what if my hearers share less than this or have very little in common with me? How then can I speak with window-words?

A missionary went forth unto the field.

And when he had established himself in a suitable (Western) mission compound, then took he stock of his situation. "How shall I share my light with these children of darkness?" he inquired of himself. "This I will do. I shall announce unto the populace that upon the seventh day at the hour of eleven they should gather themselves together to give ear unto my words." And lo, it was so. And he came unto the appointed place at the chosen hour, and a few people were gathered unto him. Then opened he his mouth and spoke forth from his wisdom in the language of his fathers. But they knew not English, perceived not his meanings, and went away with laughter. "How hard their hearts, how blind their eyes," said the missionary unto himself. And he was comforted by these words.

The missionary is you and I. The problem is ours. What can we do?

Translate the WORD. 1. Into the other's native language. 2. Into the other's natural vocabulary (in his own simple dialect). 3. Into the other's own idioms, expressions, and word pictures (where we say "you make a mountain of a molehill," he may say, "you make an elephant of a flea"). 4. We must match our meaning to his meanings. If we are talking to someone who knows our language (point 1) to assume that 2-4 can be taken for granted may sabotage all shared understandings. Our meanings may not meet at all.

31

A MEETING OF MEANING

That's what communication is: *A meeting of meaning*. Communication happens when my meaning meets your meaning across a bridge of words, and they match. Or at least they overlap enough to provide significant insight to share our meanings. If I say, "chair" we may both think of a Boston rocker, or we may visualize two different chairs, the only overlap being that both have four legs, a back, and a seat. But if I meant an inflatable — or a beanbag chair, we had only the seat in common. And if you thought I was referring to the moderator in charge of the meeting we just left, then there is no overlap at all.

ENCODING AND DECODING

Words are code sounds that contain the sender's meanings. To transmit meaning, the sender encodes the idea into the words that best express it as he has experienced it. If, however, he encodes it in words that the other fails to understand, the receiver cannot decode the concept. The communicator's task is to encode his word in words the receiver can easily and accurately decode. If an artist speaks through his art, believing that art exists for its own sake he may encode his message in a code known only to himself. The communicator's first concern is the receiver. He cares little about how perfectly it is said, how flawlessly it is encoded, how beautifully expressed. He asks instead, "Is it understood? Is it said so it cannot be misunderstood? Can the hearer break my word-code, decode my meaning, and share my experience?"

For example? Can you decode this message found on a kitchen cupboard by a ten-year-old?

"Johnny. You know what will happen to you if you don't do what I told you about you know what! — Mother"

Of the 3 billion people on this planet, only two can explain the full meaning of those words. Difficult to decode? Not for Johnny.

When Christians attempt to put the good word of God's love into words, hoping to carry the whole meaning across to another, it's more than words alone can do. The meaning I experience and express will only partly overlap the meaning you supply to the words you hear me say. Unless I not only encode — but also translate.

For example, check the overlap between the sender's untranslated terms and the receiver's (man's) understandings of these words as he uses them.

Man 1 (Encoding)	**Man 2** (Decoding)
Since I got saved,	He became thrifty or religious?
I live a victorious life,	He wins all arguments.
I'm set free from sin,	He's lost interest in sex?
I've a deep settled peace,	Nothing bothers him anymore,
I never get angry and swear,	He must be lying now.
I don't smoke or drink,	No kicks,
I'm living for Jesus.	What does He have to do with this?

Is there a translator in the house?

TRANSLATION OR REPETITION?

To let the Word come through words, the Christian must translate. That's what communicating the gospel is all about — the continuous translation of the content of the gospel into the language of our own day, and into words meaningful to each particular person in our own world.

If you see your task as a repeater, then you need not translate, you simply "say it again as you've heard it said before, said it before, and hope to say it o'er and o'er."

Again, if you are trying to communicate with your own kind of people, who share your own kind of experiences, then repetition is not only a legitimate way to communicate, it may be one of the more effective ways of inculcating ideas to achieve a high recall rate.

But to communicate, we must translate.

"No," some say, "the task is to say it the same simple way in the same simple words. Use the familiar phrases people recognize. We only communicate by sharing common accepted cliches. We must use slogans. We must simplify our propositions, and saturate the listener with the repetitive phrases. Make him hear it often enough and he will accept it." That, of course, is the propagandist's platform. It has been in constant use for centuries. Hitler perfected it as an art, advertising has made it a science, Christians have borrowed it as a way of conditioning people to accept certain basic truths. Even if Christianity were primarily four facts God wants you to know, repetition would not be enough, since it tends only to reinforce ideas already accepted and trusted.

To communicate, I translate. I put the truth of experiencing Christ-in-me into freshly chosen, personally fitted words that tell the truth just as I mean it, and just as it holds meaning for me.

JESUS — THE MASTER TRANSLATOR

It is fascinating to note the absence of the religious terms, cliches, or expressions in the teaching of Jesus. He avoided the tired Rabbinic phrases of the Pharisees, choosing rather the language of the street, the field, the seaside, the kitchen, or the carpenter shop. His translation of truth into the common experiences of life has never been equaled. He translated in pictures. Parables we call them. Any follower of His, who wants to translate as He did is constantly searching for the perfect parable.

Like their Master, Christians who seek to translate look at life with double vision. They see its temporary meaning first, and its eternal meaning second. They want to let the real meaning come through to them and then through them to others.

Just as Jesus expressed truth in the common words and situations of life, so should we. The disciple who shies away from translating and takes refuge in repeating is not following his Master, he's fearing his fellowmen.

Afraid of each other, afraid of sounding a bit unorthodox, afraid of changing the time-honored words, modern disciples tend to find safety in repeating the worn-and-weary words of others.

A Dutch Christian communicator, Albert van den Heuvel, says, "Translators must be willing to do what the Christian church usually refuses to do, to recognize the unholiness of our words. Our words have a rich history, and therefore we treat them with reverence. But they are nothing more than the wrappers of the chocolate we want to eat. We have to try and find the words of our age which cover the same reality . . . and even at the risk of losing bits of the meaning involved. If you take the translation task seriously, you do not think that you can always find a word to fit the fullness of meaning acquired by an old word through the centuries. You always lose, and so you try, generation after generation, anew." [1]

EACH IN HIS OWN WORDS

You have a unique set of words, learned from your job or profession. Can you translate your experience of the love of God in Jesus into the language of your daily lifework? A basic discipline necessary for the Christian witness is to be aware of his own experience, to be able to express it simply, and to describe the real meaning it has for him.

Try it. Put your good news into new words — in the language of your own workaday life. Encode it so that a fellow workman could decode it and recognize your meaning whether he shares it or not.

(Note: The point is not to "practice every day to find some clever lines to say to let the meaning come through. . . . The point is to . . . search and pray each day to find some clearer words to say to let His message come through."

MECHANIC

Christ, the Master mechanic...

Listened while I revved up my missing, choked-up, stalling engine. "Cut the self-ignition," He said, "Lift your hood, drop the shields. Let Me overhaul the motor."

That's what I needed, total overhaul. He replaced defective parts, rebuilt the wear and tear, tuned me to run evenly, lubricated me with His love (to run smoothly), fueled me with new energy to run more powerfully, and gave me the hot spark of His Holy Spirit.

No more knocking, no stalling, no polluting, I run more efficiently, quietly, with less friction and overheating.

I'm rebuilt.

INSURANCE ADJUSTER

Christ, the Master claim adjuster...

Examined my policy, read all the hidden clauses.

Found it inadequate, actually fraudulent, and certain not to pay out.

He invited me — in fact — gave me the courage to cancel. Then He wrote me in, not on a new contract, but on His own personal policy.

Now I've total coverage (if I stay with Him). And I'd be a fool to change. He's paid my premium in full. He is head of the company (which has unlimited resources). He's also my attorney-advocate (so I'll need no suit to collect.)

And His policy is open — now. If you are interested, give Him a call.

RECORDING ENGINEER

Christ, the Master Recording Technician...

Threaded the master tape of my life into His tape deck, auditioned my performance with an uncritical ear (even though the sound was sad, the tracks all out of synchronization, the distortion ear-shattering, the noise level high).

He heard the track with my regrets, the many takes that ended in failure, the endless errors.

He looked at me for permission, then pressed the erase button. My tape ran by the Head, and came out clean. He spliced the breaks where tension had torn me.

Now He's dubbing in new songs of joy, new backgrounds of peace, new rhythms of service, new melodies of meaning. Life is making music.

SAY IT YOUR WAY

The point of putting your experience of the gospel in words of your own is not to toy with creative expression, but to stimulate clarity in self-understanding and to encourage new flexibility in the ways of explaining the difference Jesus Christ is making in your life. That's what witness is really about — pinpointing the difference He makes.

Note the difference between you and any other person. You need no help on that. Most people are highly skilled at contrasting their strong points with their brother's weak points. Rather, it's the difference between what you are now and what you were before the power of His presence became operative in your life. It is the difference between what you are and what you would be if you were living solely by your own strength, and totally for yourself and your own satisfaction.

Say it in your own words, in your own way. Not in some prepackaged form designed by someone else to speak for someone else's experience.

There are those "witnesses" who, functioning as repeaters, have accepted a neat pattern for "the presentation" they make of the good news.

Bernie Wiebe describes this trap of a stereotyped gospel "sales presentation."

> "There are those whose message you can guess as soon as they have spoken the first sentence. It all follows a very neat pattern. If the evangelist begins with a statement of his own salvation and how he became a Christian, he is likely to follow this by pointing out that all men are sinners. Since all men are sinners, all need salvation. Salvation is provided in Jesus Christ. By believing in and receiving Christ, all men can become Christians.
>
> While this may express one formula for people to become Christians, it is very doubtful that this formula results in a sharing of faith." [2]

To share your own faith you must say it from your experience, your own normal conversational style, using your own daily vocabulary.

Any attempt to "tell it quickly, all in one dosage, in capsule form, by special formula," is handicapped from the start.

At its worst, it may be a way of unloading the "all things" on his doorstep quickly so that the responsibility for his soul is off me ("no blood on my hands"). Or it can be a way of satisfying my own ego by letting me feel that I did my part well ("I made salvation plain and simple for him"). Or it has often been a way of discharging my collected feelings of guilt in one stroke of verbal lightning ("I sure feel better now that I've done my duty").

At its best (and there are appropriate times, and valid reasons for using simplified concentrated outlines of "here's how") it is still less genuine, less believable, less personal, and less vulnerably human than just telling it like it is to me.

AWARENESS COMES WITH EXPRESSION

If you find it impossible to tell it as it happens in your life, that may only indicate how much you need the spiritual discipline of expressing your experience in concrete terms. Often you know — and yet you don't know — what your own experience of God actually is and means to you.

Dr. Paul Tournier, the Swiss Christian psychiatrist, explains why.

"We become fully conscious only of what we are able to express to someone else. We may already have had a certain inner intuition about it, but it must remain vague so long as it is unformulated."[3]

Is it safe to conclude that "we are only fully aware of what we can or have expressed to another"? Is it true that a person only knows the word of new life in Christ if he can or when he has spoken it to another? Is it a fact that only what you have shared with another is real to you?

Everyone holds many assumed and accepted values (Level one), some of which are highly prized and precious (Level two). Of these precious values some few have been expressed and experienced (Level three). Maturity in life — and especially in the Christian life — comes as we are able to move more and more of our values into the third and highest category.

To truly experience the gospel, you have to express it. That is why confession plays such a significant part in forgiveness, and witness fills a crucial role in faithful discipleship. Expression in word, deed, and presence is indispensable to both.

THE WORD INTO WORDS

How then does the follower communicate the Word in his words? He doesn't. Not of himself.

Even at his best, at his most honest, a person does not control the communication of the good Word of God's love. No one can guarantee its presence in his words of witness. (His presence, I should say). That is His part, not the disciple's.

The Holy Spirit communicates Himself. At His own time. On His own terms. When He can, He does it through you. When He cannot, He does it in spite of you.

I can only express what His word is to me in my life, and pray all the while, that He will (1) give me the right words, to speak at the right moment, and (2) get the Word through in the midst of my words.

It is in the moment of witness when conversation is opening new insights for both the Christian and the not-yet-Christian, that the Holy Spirit has promised to supply His best gifts. Jesus said, "Do not be anxious how you are to speak or what you are to say; for what you are to say will be given to you in that hour; for it is not you who speak, but the Spirit of your Father speaking through you" (Mt. 10: 19, 20).

The gift of a "word of wisdom," 1 Corinthians 12:8, is available to the witness who draws on His power as he enters into dialogue, trusting the Spirit to speak the appropriate word in the exchange of words.

For the Spirit's word to happen amid your words, you must be honest. You can use clever, seductive, manipulative words that win men's hearing, that massage their feelings, that appeal to their emotions and wills. But if they are not honest words, the Holy Spirit will not honor them by communicating the good Word of God's love through them.

Paul puts it straight. "We have renounced disgraceful, underhanded ways; we refuse to practice cunning or to tamper with God's word" (2 Cor. 4:2).

For the Spirit's Word to be heard amid your words, you must be open. Candid. Speaking of actual experience. You can dispense other people's insights, describe the events of God's working in other people's lives, give secondhand stuff that has the sound of authenticity. But if it cannot be underwritten by your own signature, the Spirit of God cannot release His full evidence of transformation in you.

Paul continues, " . . . but by the open statement of the truth we would commend ourselves to every man's conscience in the sight of God." "Take me, for example," Paul would often say, "Take me as evidence if you will. See if the fingerprints of God are not all over my life." Paul was always careful to not proclaim his own righteousness. His first concern was sharing Christ. "For what we preach is not ourselves, but Jesus Christ as Lord, with ourselves as your servants for Jesus' sake" (2 Cor. 4:5). "Where our lives can serve as examples of what Jesus does when we let Him be Lord, then we are truly your servants," says Paul.

For the Spirit's Word to be given among my words, I must be vulnerable. The power of Christ is made perfect — or is most perfectly shown — not in my strength but in my weakness. "My grace is sufficient for you," the Holy Spirit assured Paul in one of his greatest moments of vulnerability, "for my power is made perfect in weakness. . . . For the sake of Christ, then," Paul concludes, "I am content with weaknesses . . . for when I am weak, then I am strong" (2 Cor. 12:9, 10).

"The treasure of Christ is contained in pots of clay," Paul concludes. What could be more vulnerable?

A believer can profess perfectionism, pretending a maturity and an infallibility which he passes off as God in him. But the Spirit of God gives His word best through vulnerable people who accept the risks of being their true selves; confessing people who admit their humanity; repenting people who are open with their apologies, earnest in their regrets, sincere in their efforts to change; and through humble people who, recognizing the great love of God, can afford to be their true selves before others.

> Brothers,
> I did not give you
> The witness of God
> In lofty words of wisdom.
>
> I gave the Jesus word.
> The vulnerable word of weakness.
> God dead on an executioner's cross.
> And I too was weak.
>
> You saw my fears, my trembling.
> My speech was not in overpowering wisdom.
> But remember, brothers,
> The word of the Spirit was heard.
> There was power — the power of God.
> — Paraphrased from 1 Corinthians 2:1-5.

For the Spirit-Word to be present in **my** words, I must be authentic; not authoritarian, but authentic. Authority is not something I can claim, or pretend. Authority is what is perceived in the communication process. Jesus did not claim authority in communication with others, only in commissioning others. He spoke truth. He personified truth. He was truth. And they recognized the authority that is always present when truth is spoken. We could attempt to claim that authority, but it is fruitless. We are always tempted to demand the hearing for the gospel which it deserves, but it only gets the hearing I can win for it.

The follower's task is to be authentic. To be the truth. To be real. To be His. To bear witness to the One who is truth.

To let the Word — Him — come through you.

He is the real communicator, not you.

(This is no excuse for me to do less than my very best in translation and in communication, but in the final end my confidence is in the Holy Spirit.)

He puts the Word — the good Word of God's love — into my words.

For Discussion

1. If you encode your message in words the hearer does not understand, what does it communicate to him? "You are not important to us?" "You probably wouldn't understand anyway?" "If you learn our language, we'll talk to you?"
2. If you really trusted the Holy Spirit to do something on His own in other people's hearts, would you be less compulsive, less directive and authoritarian in witness, more winsome and attractive?
3. Is it true that your own "before and after" story, told simply and in straightforward speech, is your most powerful witness?
4. Do you remember what was said by anyone who helped you to Christ? Or were you won more by what they were to you? And did you feel drawn by what they were (nonverbal communication) even in spite of what they said (verbal communication)?

5. If you truly translate the good news into your own words — from your own experience — what will you say to those who protest, "You didn't say all from A to Z, you left out to K to Q and V to X"?

For Assignment

1. Write out your testimony as you've always thought it, then translate it into at least two different sets of words — your on-the-job vocabulary, your family relationship words, or your favorite hobby talk. As you write, think of someone who knows those words but does not know Christ. Share your translation with him or her, tell him what you're doing, ask him to improve it. Put it in electrical terms, show it to your electrician, etc.
2. Pick six of your favorite phrases: "Christ is the answer." "Accept Jesus as Savior and Lord," etc. Ask a non-Christian friend to tell you, off the cuff in free association, what they mean when he hears them. (Don't you explain them unless he asks.)
3. Find three parables which illustrate the good news in the ordinary things of life. Jot them down to share in class. If you have difficulty seeing such things, read *Prayers*, by Michel Quoist, Sheed and Ward Publishers.

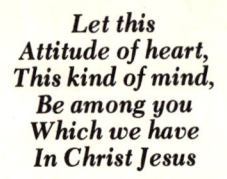

*Let this
Attitude of heart,
This kind of mind,
Be among you
Which we have
In Christ Jesus*

*He was always
God by nature*

*All to the glory
Of God the Father*

*Yet He did not
Grasp at equality
Of rights with God*

*Every tongue
Shall confess,
"Jesus is Lord"*

*But laid aside
All privilege*

*All in heaven,
On earth, or under the earth
Shall praise Him*

*Emptied Himself,
Took the form
Of a slave*

*That at the name
Jesus,
Every knee shall bow*

*Was born
A mortal man*

*And gave Him
A name above all names*

*As a man
He humbled himself
To a life of obedience*

*But now God
Has lifted Him up.
Exalting Him highly*

*And died
The death
Of a common
Criminal*

Phil. 2:4-11

WHAT THE GOSPEL IS

The Good News for the Whole Man

3

*God
Came.
In person.
In the flesh.
In humanity.
He
Became
Man,
He felt
What we feel.
He hurt
Where we hurt.
He died
Like we die.
He knows.
He knows us.*

Witness.
Service.
Presence.

How do we give the good news?

Where do we begin? In witness? In service? In presence? In all three at once? Or in the need of the moment?

"Witness and service are the two sides of the Christian coin," John Yoder once said, breaking in on our small-group argument over evangelism and social concern. He took a coin from his pocket. "Now which comes first, heads — evangelism or tails — service? Let's see which is most important. Heads side says, 'In God we trust.' That's the good news from the treasury, if it were only true. It also says, 'liberty,' true for a few, it says '1964,' no longer true. But the tails side gives the worth, 'twenty-five cents,' says who stands behind it, 'the United States.' So which is most important? The side that says 'what' or the side that says 'why'?" Neither, he concluded, it's the coin itself that matters. So neither social concern nor evangelism is all important, it's the coin itself, the new creation in Christ.

48

Christians seem to insist on polarizing when this comes up for discussion. It's hard to see the whole new creation in the viewpoints they defend. They force a contrast between the so-called "social gospel" and "simple gospel," between the "activist" and the "pietist," the "man of action" and the "man of devotion," between practical and spiritual, liberal and conservative, witness and service.

Elton Trueblood, in his book *The New Man for Our Time*, points out how false this tension between the two actually is.

"The polarization of our time, which produces half men who could be whole men, may be made vivid by reference to both the roots and the fruits of Christian faith. The pietist is one who stresses chiefly the roots; the activist is one who stresses chiefly the fruits. Service without devotion is rootless, devotion without service is fruitless. The necessity of stressing each of these without at the same time neglecting the other is abundantly clear in the recorded teaching of Christ Himself. He was certainly presenting the necessity, though not the sufficiency, of human service when He said repeatedly in the Sermon on the Mount, 'You will know them by their fruits' (Mt. 7:16, 20). But He was also presenting the balancing truth when He said, 'Since it had no root it withered away'" (Mk. 4:6).[1]

"The new man for our time is the whole man, the man who consciously rejects the temptation to limit himself to one part of a totality, when such limitation is not required."[2]

CHRIST THE WORD AND THE WAY

The pattern for wholeness in personhood, in integrity, in witness, and in service is Jesus Christ. He alone demonstrates for us whole concern and whole compassion for the whole man.

Christ is not only the content of our gospel — the message. Christ is also our pattern — the method.

Christ is not only our communication, but He is also the way to communicate.

He is both our Word and our way. And He alone. I cannot communicate the Jesus-word unless I do it in the Jesus-way.

"As the Father has sent me, even so I send you," Jesus said to His disciples. Jesus was commissioned by the Father to incarnate love and to communicate that love. If His commission to you is modeled after the one He received from His Father, then your obedience to that commission should be patterned after His own obedience. His way must be your way.

The Jesus-way of giving the Word must be the way. You go about fulfilling His commission to "go, teach, baptize, and build a community of love."

INCARNATIONAL EVANGELISM

The incarnation, life teaching, and work of Christ is meant to be the Christian's pattern. For a statement like that to carry meaning across to daily living, it must be translated. Incarnation means enfleshing. To put God's Word into human form, to express it in human terms, to live it out in a human body. To flesh out the truth of God in the grubby interchange of the workbench or the marketplace.

Incarnation to the Christian carries the additional meaning of one who is fully God who became truly man to live among men. For that reason, many shrink from applying this word to their own fleshing-out of the gospel. So people substitute words to express the nature of the Christian's presence in the world, and sometimes the concept is almost lost completely. Because the truth is, there are no substitute words for incarnation. It cannot be translated into a single word. It demands a minimum of three.

Identification.   Demonstration.   Affirmation.

These are the three dimensions of Christ's incarnation, and the three dimensions of the Christian commission to continue fleshing out God's good Word of love. All three are necessary. All three must be present, all three are equally crucial.

The "servant-song" with which Paul celebrated the incarnation of Christ in his letter to the Philippians (2: 5-10), will be the biblical base for exploring these dimensions.

IDENTIFICATION

When God became a man, He didn't hesitate, He came all the way down. All the way. At once. Then He reached out. During His time among us, He did no reaching down. There was no attitude of condescension. (That famous Christmas sermon "The Divine Condescension" missed the good news.) No condescension. No air of superiority. No "hand-down," or "hand-out" attitudes in Jesus.

He first became one of us. One of the little people. One of the poor. We have glibly said, "God became man." But the truth is, "God became a poor man."

The natural habitat of God is the slum.

He identified with us, by taking our identity for His own (v. 7).

"He emptied himself," Paul says (v. 7), describing the great step Christ took in identification. He laid aside not just His natural rights of equality with God, but all rights, privileges, and powers of deity. He lived a life of dependent obedience. Whatever unique powers in signs, wonders, or miracles that He displayed during His life, they were given Him of God because of His perfect obedience (v. 8 and

Hebrews 5:8) qualified Him to receive the Spirit of God without measure — with no limitations. (See John 3:34, 35.) Like you and me, the Son lived in utter day-to-day dependence upon the Father. Unlike us, His perfect obedience allowed Him to be used of God — through the Spirit — with no limitations whatsoever.

But make no mistake. He was truly human. In complete identification with us. No Jupiter in human masquerade, no superman in street clothes. There was total identification.

We hesitate to believe the full truth of this. We recoil from a God who comes downward because all our thoughts are of climbing upward. We want to be great, to compete with God. "The proud man is a grotesque caricature of God," St. Augustine once wisely observed. In man's pretentions of perfection, his illusions of superiority (shown by paternalistic attitudes of helping others by reaching down) men do not compete with God, they contradict God. Man in vanity, strives to move upward. God in humility comes downward in identification. The upward/downward movements clashed at Calvary. God accepted defeat, in humility, then broke out of the grave in divine virility.

The way of Jesus for the disciple is a way of identification with all those for whom Christ died, with whom He identified.

William Stringfellow, in his book *My People Is the Enemy,* writes his conclusions from the early years of his practice as an attorney in New York where he lived in a walk-up tenement in East Harlem.

"To become and to be a Christian is, therefore, to have the extraordinary freedom to share the burdens of the daily, common, ambiguous, transient, perishing existence of men, even to the point of actually taking the place of another man, whether he be powerful or weak, in health or in sickness, clothed or naked, educated or illiterate, secure or persecuted, complacent or despondent, proud or forgotten, housed or homeless, fed or hungry, at liberty or in prison, young or old, white or Negro, rich or poor."[3] This state of being truly identified, is called "solidarity." Solidarity is the basis of incarnational love, not love's final result; Christlike love grows.

Peter Dyck has written on this: "The first requisite for Christian service is not love, but solidarity with the world. Love without solidarity is nothing else but spiritual pride. I am first of all a person like other persons — Catholics, Muslims, or communists. Where this solidarity is denied or played down, there is also good reason to question the quality of the love."[4]

The solidarity which Jesus expressed was as generous as grace. He healed the slave of the Roman soldier without asking the military man to lay down his weapons or resign his commission and become something other than an enemy oppressor. Solidarity loves without drawing lines. It identifies without setting conditions. That's why solidarity is so impossibly hard. It loves with no strings attached. Jesus died for the disciples who had betrayed, denied, and abandoned Him to His executioners. He died also for the calloused soldiers, the corrupt politicians, the close-minded men of the cloth.

He was truly "a friend of sinners." Could that be said of you?

To follow Christ in identification is to empty myself of the pride that holds me apart from others, to deny myself and take the *solidare* way of the cross, and live for others as Jesus did. To identify, I listen, I hear, I feel with the other. I love.

DEMONSTRATION

"God did not become a poor man just for the hell of

it," Archbishop William Temple once said (likely the one time he used such language in his entire life), "not for the hell of it, but to lead us out of the hell of evil we have made."

God came in Jesus, to flesh out His love in believable acts of human kindness, in the credible deeds of loving service.

But make no mistake, the incarnation was no tactical maneuver, the acts of service were not strategies to coerce men to His way. He gave Himself unreservedly so that men might live. He gave out neither charity nor pity, He lived a daily demonstration of love that left men with their dignity intact.

He became "a slave by nature . . . humbled himself by living a life of utter obedience, even to the extent of dying."[5] So J. B. Phillips translates Philippians 2:6, 7.

As a servant, Jesus was truly a man for others. He could be the man for others — which means primarily being a servant to others — because He Himself was a man of God. He demonstrated God's love by helping when and how help was needed, not primarily to indoctrinate or to convert men to a set of doctrines based on a necessary set of assumptions and propositions, but to show them what life, truly lived for God and for others, can be.

As a servant, Jesus fulfilled the ancient prophecy of Isaiah in utter perfection. Since the Spirit of God was upon Him without measure, since in Godlike humility He lived in flawless obedience to God the Father, He could demonstrate God's servant-image of what man should be.

"The Spirit of the Lord is upon me,.
Because he anointed me to preach good tidings to the poor:
He hath sent me to proclaim release to the captives,
And recovering of sight to the blind,
To set at liberty them that are bruised,

To proclaim the acceptable year of the Lord."

And so He could say, "This very day this scripture has been fulfilled, while you have been listening to it"[6] (Lk. 4: 18-21, Phillips)!

"To preach good tidings . . . to proclaim release . . . recovering of sight, to set at liberty . . . to proclaim." To demonstrate as He proclaims. It is not an either/or matter.

Missions leader and bishop Lesslie Newbigin has an incisive word on this.

"Our Lord was sent both to preach and to be servant to all. . . . Each of these two activities has its proper dignity within the wholeness of the mission, and neither should be subordinated to the other. If service is made merely ancillary to evangelism, then deeds which should be pure acts of love and compassion become suspect as having an ulterior motive. When our Lord stretched forth His hand to heal a leper, there was no evangelistic strategy attached to the act. It was a pure outflow of the divine love into the word, and needed no further justification.

"On the other hand, if evangelism is subordinated to programs of service, if there is no faith in the supernatural power of the living word to bring forth fruit a hundredfold, then the church is guilty of the folly of turning from the Spirit to the flesh . . . if these two things cannot be subordinated the one to the other, neither can they be separated. Preaching unaccompanied by deeds of love that authenticate it, becomes in the end an empty sound; and service which does not explicitly point men to Christ Himself, ultimately mocks men with false securities."[7]

Jesus demonstrated the truth that He spoke in unforgettable acts. He knew the power of the deed to communicate meanings which words may not be able to express.

His acts — the many healing touches, the attentive listening ear given the Samaritan woman, the dinner engagements with Pharisees, tax collectors, or ex-prostitutes, the angry scene in the temple, or the silence of the refusal to testify in self-defense. Or Calvary. Such acts cut across all cultural barriers.

Mahatma Gandhi, like Christ, knew the eloquence of simple acts. His choice to live in poverty spoke his solidarity with the masses of India, as no words could have. (One of his aides once commented that "it was fantastically expensive to keep Gandhi living in such obvious poverty, but it was his most powerful communication.") Or take his salt march to the sea in protest of British tariffs on foodstuffs. It was nonsense to walk to the ocean and distill a few spoonfuls of salt, but it said to a people divided horizontally by a many-layered caste system and vertically by many different language and racial groups that they could stand together.

Think of the greatest witnesses to Jesus Christ, past or present. All of them demonstrated the truth they spoke in vivid deed.

Demonstration is not only a Father Damien serving his leper congregation until he addresses them "we lepers."

It is Clarence Jordan forgetting danger at Koinonia Farms. It is Martin Luther King sitting on the first empty seat of a bus that Montgomery, Alabama, morning. It is Clayton Kratz (MCC worker who disappeared in Russia), Daniel Gerber, Ted Studebaker (Christian service workers who died or disappeared in Vietnam). It is Nevin Bender rebuilding Nanih Waiya Mennonite Church a third time; it is Tabor Community Services in Lancaster; it is Hubert Schwartzentruber putting people above the things most citizens of St. Louis value. It is . . . (I'm suddenly aware that I've started something I can't finish. The list of powerful demonstrations of truth in life in the Jesus way of service is crowding everything else out of my mind. I could finish the next fifty pages of this book simply reporting on people, places, and deeds of love.)

Where there is power in giving the Jesus word in a living way, that word is being demonstrated in a way of life.

This is the Jesus-way: to identify in solidarity, to demonstrate in humility, and to affirm with simplicity.

AFFIRMATION

Examine the servant-song a third time.

He took the form of man, emptying Himself in identification,

He took the form of a slave, humbling Himself in gentle service,

He died — the cross affirmed the truth of all His affirmations in word and deed.

Man rejected Him, refused to recognize Him. But God speaks in affirmation, giving Him a name above all names. And the day will come when every voice in creation will affirm that He is Lord.

Like our Lord, like our Father, we too affirm the truth in Jesus.

Somewhere — I wish I could say where — the late Daniel T. Niles wrote: "Our deeds cannot take the place of our Word, because the Word we have to give is always greater than ourselves."

We also affirm — if we give the good news that meets man's need in the Jesus-way — we also affirm the truth which is at the center. Jesus is that truth.

Christians do not assist their brothers with food, housing, agricultural know-how, education, literacy, and medical treatment just so they can save a soul. But as believers assist in a, b, c, and d, they affirm that a person can be saved as a whole person and receive eternal life.

Evangelism is the commitment that whatever a Christian is and does will be motivated by concern for the other's eternal life in Christ. Whatever the Christian does, he does to facilitate the work of the Spirit for the salvation of those about him.

Not that he serves with strings attached. Peter Dyck is helpful again at this point.

"Service is Christian when there are no strings attached. The calculated stance . . . [of helping another to help ourselves] does not become any more sanctified when the intention is to win people to the church or Jesus Christ. Bait is bait and tactical maneuver is just that regardless how piously expressed. Service that recognizes the worth and dignity of a person will never exploit another — least of all for the sake of winning him to Christ. It is simply another case of ends not justifying means. But service that is Christian seeks to generate faith in God. This is not a string attached. Seeking to generate faith in God is a recognition that man's needs are not all physical, that he does not live by bread alone. When there are strings, these are attached to the service or the gift in such a way that the recipient is not free, he is like a fish caught by bait on a line. . . . But when one seeks to generate faith in God, that is not an attempt to pull the recipient to oneself but to bring him into a meaningful relationship to God. The intent is not some benefit for the servant, but a greater benefit to the recipient."[8]

To seek, in the Jesus way, to be used by the Holy Spirit in the conversion of another can be a totally unselfish act. Our affirmations of the life-changing power of Jesus can be given freely and clearly without pressuring and coercing.

You can clearly affirm the truth without slipping into the dogmatic arrogance that assumes that you can become an authority for another. Soren Kierkegaard, the Danish philosopher, once wrote, "No human being was ever truly an authority for another, or ever helped anyone by posing as such."

Authority is not something to be claimed by the witness. He simply affirms the truth as he knows it. When God is present in the relationship and in the words spoken, authority is present too.

Authority is something the hearer recognizes. He must sense it, recognize it for himself. (As did Jesus' hearers.) The person must be able to perceive truth for himself. To tell him the truth will not make him see. When Pilate asked Jesus: "What is truth?" Jesus did not answer. The answer could not be put in words. The answer was, obviously: "The truth stands before you. I am the truth." But such truth cannot just be told. If Pilate cannot recognize truth, no amount of telling will help him.[9]

When you witness you affirm the truth about Jesus, but without shading the facts as you know them. How else could you be responsible to the most basic fact of all — that there is only one way to God — Jesus?

Howard Lowry, the late president of Wooster College, told of a fascinating conversation with Dr. Radhakrishnan, the Hindu philosopher who became president of India. Dr. Lowry had just remarked that he was sometimes embarrassed by the Christian claim of the uniqueness of Jesus Christ. To say to India, where only ten million out of four hundred million are Christians, "Jesus Christ is *the* light of the world," seems arrogant, like saying, "We alone have the light."

Dr. Radhakrishnan paused for a moment of reflection, and then replied, "Yes, but the Christian has no choice. This is what your Scriptures say; you cannot say less. You are saved from arrogance when you say it in the Spirit of Jesus Christ."[10]

The Jesus way is affirming the truth in loving respect for the other person.

Identification, that sits alongside others in loving solidarity, does not hesitate to demonstrate that love in selfless service, and hurries to affirm the meaning and power of it all.

All these are necessary. The three are indivisible. The three together comprise the way of Jesus.

Fragmenting the gospel includes *affirmation* without *demonstration* and/or *identification*.

There are those who complain that witness and affirmation twist Christian service out of its true shape as a lovely and unselfish end in itself, and debase it into a cold, calculating tool of proselytism. It is no prostitution of the Jesus-way of loving service to identify its source, its model, its power supply. It is only a perversion when by word or work we accept the credit for ourselves.

All three dimensions of the Jesus-way are authentic and worthy in themselves, but none of them is sufficient by itself. There is no sequence, they are simultaneous acts of obedience. The witness begins where the need is, in any one, two, or all three of these aspects of giving the good word of Jesus.

This is fleshing out the Jesus-word — is it not — in the Jesus-way?

This is giving the good news that meets the whole need of the whole man, to bring the whole man to Christ.

For Discussion
1. Is there any value in debating which is more important: identification (presence) demonstration (service), and affirmation (witness)? Or are they all three necessary at all times?
2. Is there any order in sequence of these three dimensions of living the Jesus-way? Or should all three always be simultaneous? Or do we begin where the other has need and move as rapidly as possible to the third? Can one witness spend his whole life in dimension one, or two, and still be faithful? What about missions in countries such as Somalia where only one and two are openly possible?
3. What are the greatest needs in your community? (1) for Christians to identify and be truly present rather than withdrawn? (2) for you to show the love of Jesus in service, deed, or action? Do you need more "Compassion Fund projects," "Day Care Centers"? (3) are people prepared and hungry to hear, "How to be forgiven and set free in Jesus"?

For Assignment
1. Call a local parole officer, welfare department head, social worker, visiting teacher, and ask, "If there were ten Christians eager to assist in simple, loving service to others, willing for any assignment, what would you have to suggest?" Bring your findings to class.
2. Consider a seven-day experiment, to live — to enflesh — the Jesus-way as you understand it now to your fullest ability right where you are. Identify. Give the gift of open presence. Demonstrate. Show love in believable ways. Witness. Tell it like it is in your own life. Give your good intentions a thorough experiment.

*Can
I give you
My word?
No, it is not
My word
That I have to give.
It is His Word,
That must be spoken.*

*Can
I do it
In my own way?
No, not really.
He is the way.
His word
Must be given
In His own way.*

*Can
I tell it
Like I see it?
No, not quite.
His truth
Is greater than
Any insight
I have found.*

*And
Yet
To give
The Jesus-word
In the Jesus-way,
I still must
Give you my word,
In my own way,
Tell it as I see it.*

*But I must try
To stay out of sight,
To get out of the way,
To let Him be seen and heard,
To let Him be Word, and Way, and Truth
Even in me.*

HOW TO COMMUNICATE IT
Giving the Jesus-Word in the Jesus-Way

4

*The
Jesus-word,
"Grace,"
Is to be given
In the
Jesus-way,
"Grace."*

*To receive
"Grace"
Is to
Know
That you
Are accepted,
Even when
You know
That you are
Unacceptable.*

*To extend
"Grace"
Is to
Give
Acceptance,
Accepting even
The unacceptable.
"Freely we received,
Freely we must give."*

What a strange witness — this Jesus.

His first word was, "Repent and turn, turn, turn!"

But His first act? He asked for baptism. He stood in the line of repentant sinners in the ankle-deep mud of the Jordan, identified Himself with those who came confessing and receiving the grace of God, and God graced Him with a sign of His power. He identified with men — with the humble, honest men.

His first friends? Little people. The poor. The castoffs, the dropouts, the rejects of society. He was like that. "A friend of sinners," not of "saints." And the sinners loved

Him, followed Him, and from them He chose His disciples. The "saints" haunted the fringes of His life, shadowed His movement among the people. The "saints" taunted Him with questions, rejected His answers before they heard them, and finally killed Him.

Strange, is it not? The sick, the sad, the failures, the no-goods adore Him. And the good people can't stand Him!

And He witnessed in such strange ways.

He listened. Listened to man and woman alike. He loved them with His listening. There's the instance of the outcast, minority group prostitute from the Samaritan ghetto. He listened to her, drew her out, listened until she was liberated from her past and saw "everything she ever did" in the new light of forgiveness.

He was gentle with those who were weak, tender with those who grew slowly, patient where understanding and action were late in coming. He would plant the seed and wait long for life to spring up. He could satisfy the request, "Lord, that I might receive my sight" and wait for the second question, "Who art Thou, Lord?" He was careful to respect the freedom of each person to choose or refuse. He did not threaten, force, or coerce. He honored the dignity of each person and personality.

And yet, to the man at the threshold of decision, He could state the alternatives with striking clarity and uncompromising honesty. He could demand the best of a man of action, incisively, unhesitatingly. And to those who had hardened themselves against the truth, He could be embarrassingly, sharply, scathingly honest.

He gave the witness of God. And men saw that it was true. Some chose to follow. Some feared Him, and fled. If the Jesus-way of witness strikes us as strange, we had best go back to the Book in careful study of the Jesus-way of giving "the good Word of God's love."

TENDER — RESPECTFUL — LOVE

It is fascinating to observe how Paul reminisces back through his experience of witness to the citizens of Thessalonica. Read it for yourself in 1 Thessalonians 2:1-13.

" . . . our motives are pure . . ."

" . . . our conduct is absolutely aboveboard . . ."

" . . . we speak under the solemn sense of being entrusted by God with the Gospel . . ."

" . . . we do not aim to please men, but to please God . . ."

" . . . no one could ever say . . . we used flattery to conceal greedy motives . . ."

" . . . God himself is witness to our honesty . . ."

" . . . our attitude among you was of tenderness . . . like that of a devoted nurse among her babies . . ."

" . . . it was a joy to us to give you not only the Gospel of God but our very hearts — so dear did you become to us . . ."

" . . . our life among you believers was honest, straightforward and above criticism . . ."

" . . . we dealt with each one of you personally, like a father with his own children . . ."

"When you heard . . . the Word of God you accepted it, not as a mere human message, but as it really is, God's Word, a power in the lives of you who believe" (1 Thess. 2:3-13).[1]

The Jesus-way of giving the good Word of God's love is "tender, honest, compassionate, personal," it is given in love.

There are many facets to this love. A person can say it in different acts and words.

To say, "I hear you, I hear where you really are" is to give an understanding ear.

To say, "I feel with you. I hurt where you are hurting," is to give heart, call it empathy or call it concern, it's heart.

To say, "I recognize you, I affirm your dignity as a free person," is to give respect, to be a responsible brother to another.

To say, "I am open to share with you, I am open to receive from you," is to love and to be loved. The real test of the maturity of one's love is the ability to graciously and humbly receive a gift from another.

To explore the Jesus-way of giving His word, let's examine each of these statements and stances.

"I HEAR YOU, I HEAR WHERE YOU ARE."

Love begins by truly hearing another. There is a great joy that comes to you at the moment when you are truly heard by another. It's a liberating joy, a freedom that is deeply felt when someone else hears you without judging, without taking responsibility for you, without trying to remake or remold you into their image. They simply hear you, hear your hurts and frustrations, share the burden of them for the moment, and say in that act, "I hear you, I accept you, I do not turn away from you."

Loving others, in the Jesus-way, is extending this liberating quality of deep hearing to the other person. It is giving him or her the gift of a loving, open, understanding human ear. That is when you give him or her the ear to your soul. Listening with "soul" is listening to the whole person. To the words, the feeling tones, the thoughts he cannot quite express, to the conscious or the unconscious meanings that keep coming through, to the deep human cry that is reaching out to you, the silent scream that may be buried and unknown.

Listening, in the Jesus-way, is loving the other enough to try to receive the message that he is, on all the levels that he is trying to speak. When it happens, you can see it in the other's eyes. There's a gratefulness called trust. A moistness in the eyes that signals the tears of joy.

To say it in parable.

It's like a miner trapped in a cave, or a prisoner isolated for months in solitary confinement. At last the lonely person devises a signal which he can tap on the wall. Finally, he hears an answering rap of his improvised morse code. He raps again to be sure. Then hears the identical taps. Suddenly he is numb with joy. "I've been heard. Someone knows that I am. Someone knows that I am alive."

That same joy breaks over another when he has been truly heard. "Someone else knows what it is to be me, inside this unacceptable self. With all my unexplainable problems, someone has heard me and did not turn away."

That is love. Not in word, so much, as in deed. Such listening is a loving deed of "burden-bearing" as Paul might have called it. When a person has been heard, and feels understood, he is able to see his world in a new way, he gains a different perspective that helps him move a step toward change. Not that we change him; but in listening, healing may begin that makes the insolvable become solvable, the unbearable now bearable. Perhaps it begins as the listener, for a few moments, shoulders the load for the other person. In the moment's space, he gets a second wind to pick up the load again.

To be able to say, "I hear you, I hear where you are" by the simple acts of listening (so that you do not need to say it in words), is the first step in the Jesus-way of relating to others.

"I FEEL WITH YOU, I HURT WHERE YOU HURT."

To say, "I hurt where you hurt," in words is no more believable than the classic, "This is going to hurt me more than it hurts you" line fathers are supposed to use before punishing a child.

It cannot be said, but it must be told. In deed. In spirit. In the attitude of heart that comes through in what you are.

It begins for you when you feel with the other person, through empathy, the anguish or frustration that is causing them pain. You learn to see things from the other person's frame of reference.

To say it in parable:

It is like a man who is trying desperately to kick the habit of smoking. Mark Twain confesses, "Quitting smoking is the easiest thing in the world. I've done it a thousand times. It's staying quit that's hard." So he locks himself in his bedroom, throws the key out through the transom, tells his wife he's going to stay in seven days and break it "cold turkey." Her part is to toss him his daily sandwich — preferably not cold turkey — through the transom, and refuse to return the key. By the second day he is climbing the walls, dry-mouthed and sweat-studded. Then in the corner he finds an old ashtray. Feverishly he sorts through the contents — thirty-six butts. A pack of matches. He places them end to end. Every six butts rolled in tissue will make a cigarette. With thirty-six butts, six butts to a "cig." How many will it make?

Nonsmokers invariably answer "six." Smokers who have lived the panic of no-pack-in-the-pocket answer just as quickly "seven." They know from deep involvement that when the first six are smoked they will have six butts left for the seventh.

That is the difference between distantly hearing-the-other, and being truly present, feeling-with-the-other.

To view another's life — as far as it is possible — from within, requires a deep kind of hearing beyond hearing. It is only possible in a fragmentary sort of way. But those fragments of insight, puzzling though they may be, can piece together a different kind of picture, a different vision of who and what the other truly is. The picture is helpful, not so much as a means of mapping out the other's personality, as it is in protecting us from judging and typecasting the other person. To attempt to feel for another from inside out is not a way of judging, of understanding the other. Rather it is an earnest attempt to understand without judging.

To love another in the Jesus-way, is to care for another "as a nurse with children," as "a father with a son." Where the other person feels pain or passion, we experience common-passion or compassion.

"I RECOGNIZE YOU. I AFFIRM YOUR DIGNITY AS A FREE PERSON."

This is the real goal. To affirm the other person's worth — supreme worth in God's sight — to say by all that we are, "God loves you, you are loved, God is for you, you can be new."

The Christian witness is not a super sleuth, listening skillfully, deciphering brilliantly, sniffing out others' frailties, sins, and failures. That is not the goal.

The goal of living the Jesus-way is to affirm the value of people. We begin to affirm the worth of others by listening with love so that they are freed to express where they really are.

We grow in affirmation of another by feeling with him, crying with him, hurting with him to assure him that his emotions are valid, understandable, acceptable.

We truly affirm the other when we extend forgiveness to him or her. When he feels that you forgive, he is freed to confess in an open released way. "No one ever truly confesses until he senses the possibility of forgiveness in another," John Calvin somewhere writes. It is true that a person is only able to express the real meaning of sin when he knows forgiveness is reaching out to him. We free another to confess, not by urging him "to make a clean breast, to get it all out in the open, etc.," but by sitting silently in prayer, asking the Lord Jesus that His Spirit will reach out in forgiveness to assure the other that he will be accepted and loved even as he admits where and what he is.

Often Christians value their effectiveness by the good words they've said. But it is not so much what they say but what happens in the loving chemistry of the Holy Spirit in their relationships together. To affirm the worth of another in God's sight is to be a messenger of the good news to that person.

"I AM OPEN TO SHARE WITH YOU."

As Christians listen, empathize, and affirm the worth of others they also affirm where they stand. I tell who and what I am in Jesus Christ. I witness to the presence of Jesus in my life.

In all that a believer is and does, he wants to let Him — our Lord Jesus — be seen, felt, experienced, expressed; however, it should be said that we want to let His presence be real through our openness to share life with the other person.

So you openly share the life you are experiencing at that moment as a gift from Jesus. You tell what He did, why He does it, where He is doing it now. You share His witness, you do not try to force it on another. You do not coerce or cajole. You are witnesses, not arm twisters; witnesses, not soul-winners. (That is an Old Testament phrase taken from a mistranslation of a proverb. Read Proverbs 11:30 in the Revised Standard Version.)

You share the good news in such a way that you can be a small part of that good news to the other person.

WHAT IS THIS WAY OF WITNESSING?

It is being a co-worker with the Holy Spirit.

All human forms of persuasion are based on one person's ability to be attractive, influential, magnetic, or domineering. But that is not the Christian way. The Holy Spirit is power, not a man with his cleverness, or his busy words. He is that power. And not necessarily through us. More often in spite of us.

Silence is the first step. The silence that trusts the Spirit to be speaking. Often the most powerful moments of witness are unmarred with words. Christians sit silently together as they pray and wait for the Spirit to move in the seeker's heart. No one ever talked or scared anyone into rebirth. Persuasion is a work of the Holy Spirit. As the Danish Christian Soren Kierkegaard once ordered: "Silence! Bring about silence! God's word cannot be heard." "Be still and know," David said.

Often people attempt to do the Holy Spirit's work for Him. ("He takes too long," the anxious think, "He is too slow. He may not be able to convince or convict unless I do it. I must convert the sinner.")

But I am not a spiritual midwife, nor a soul-obstetrician. That is the Holy Spirit's work. I have often caused a spiritual miscarriage, on occasion an abortion, or a stillbirth, in my impatience. His timing is perfect.

Perhaps this point is best made in parable.

As a boy I made an incubator of an old box and a hundred-watt bulb. A half dozen chicken eggs were placed inside and rotated under the gentle warmth twice a day. After a dozen days, my curiosity was uncontrollable. I broke an egg to see if there was progress. There was, but the life was soon snuffed out. Sixteen, seventeen, nineteen days passed. The time for hatching came close. I couldn't wait. At the first sign of life breaking through, I had to help. I flaked away the shell in eager helpfulness. Only to be bitterly disappointed. No matter how well intentioned my efforts, the chicks died. Only those who answered to their own time signals, who came to their own moment of birth, who struggled through all the difficulties of breaking out, came to life.

The Christian's task is not to give help, but to give love. His work is not to attack the egg with hammer and pliers but to gently warm it.

David Redding had an excellent word on this in *Christianity Today*, some years ago.

"Rebirth cannot be predicted or scheduled. It is never accomplished through our clever leading questions. It happens after a sufficient incubation period, and all we can do to help it along is to wrap the other person in a patience that has time for him, trying our best to keep out of God's way. Meanwhile we keep our spirit of judgment busy on our own failings, which equal those of this one who has been sent to us. And if we bend low enough, we will allow him to see over us to Christ."[2]

WHY CAN'T WE HELP?

Nobody really loves helper-type people. Nobody wants to receive help from another — not as long as we can avoid it. To give help is great — and helper-type person "has his reward" even as he gives. To receive help is painful. If you offer a class on "how to give help" you will have a good enrollment. But advertise a workshop on "how to receive help" and you'll study alone.

No one wants to be helped, nor does anyone like to be served by the helper-type person who comes to his aid on his terms, by his own design to meet his own ends.

To put the problem in terse form.

One: The idea that I may help you is presumptuous since no one wants to receive help from another.

Two: Every person has the right to refuse my help.

Three: I must not only give others the right to refuse any help I may be in a position to offer, I must also let him know that I recognize and respect his right to refuse my help.

Giving help is obviously a very ticklish business. To say, "May I help you, let me be of help," is presumptuous at best, and offensive and insulting when done at its worst. This may sound strange since helping another human being sounds like such a simple process, but actually, it is one of the hardest things that anyone can be called on to do.

Help may not be wanted, and the person in need may refuse it because it hurts his pride to admit where he is, or because he doesn't want to feel indebted. Or help may be accepted, and then used in a way that seems self-defeating, or totally misused so that the person is weaker and more dependent afterward than before. Or help may be resented — whether it is accepted or refused — and the helper is rejected. So often this happens in Christian witness. The helper-type witness who attempts to take over the responsibility for the other's life and decisions finds his help, his gospel, his love, and his Christ rejected all "in one fell swoop."

So if help is to be given, it must be given in a way which respects the other's dignity as a person; respects the other's freedom as a being of responsible moral choice; respects the other's right to refuse by letting him know that you will not infringe on his freedom.

How then do you ever help another? Not by being helper-type people who insist on being changers. To change another is an unwanted service. It is inevitably judgmental, it is inherently superior and paternalistic. It is one person playing God for another.

WHAT IS HELP — HOW IS IT GIVEN?

To give help really means to offer someone an opportunity to change. To give help is to provide the freedom for another to initiate change in himself. All other help is a temporary patch up until the next break comes, necessary perhaps for the moment, but not of lasting and permanent value.

Help is good if the recipient can choose to make use of it — on his own initiative.

"This kind of choice — to choose to change — is terribly hard. It is terribly personal. And it is terribly dangerous. Truly . . . one must lose one's life to gain it. To ask someone to change is to ask the unknown.

"For making this kind of choice always means at least four things. It means admitting your own failure. It means putting one's self more or less in the power of another, letting him know you and take part in your life. It means hard work, for the choice has to be made again and again in different contexts. It means risking the unknown; giving up a present certainty, even though this may be an uncomfortable one, for a good which cannot as yet be fully seen."[3]

So writes Dr. Alan Keith-Lucas, a professor of Social Work at the University of North Carolina. Then he goes on to make an incisive comparison.

"The correspondences between asking for human help and the religious experience of conversion are so remarkable that they cannot, I feel, be entirely accidental. The words repentance, submission, steadfastness under temptation, and faith are plainly corollary to the four elements described [above]. There is one important difference. The person approaching God for help must try to submit entirely to His will . . . the person seeking human help cannot submit to the will of the helper. . . . In fact he must always maintain his integrity as a separate person, against the will of the helper . . . human will tends always to control and not to set free. Do you see why receiving help is so difficult?"[14]

To give help to another we must let him — and the Holy Spirit — be the changer. So we witness without attempting to remake and remold the person. To help, you must truly "love the other as you love yourself."

> You must want to help another
>   Without being remembered as the helper.
> You must want to benefit the other
>   Without being recognized as the benefactor.
> You must want to give to your brother
>   Without being regarded as the "Great Giver."

Helping is always a two-way interchange, it involves two people. Whatever goes wrong in the helping process may lie with either the helper, or with the way his help is extended. But it is two-way — make no mistake. To give help is to receive help, too. To share insight with another is to receive new insight. Help is always two-way.

WITNESS AND GIVING HELP

The Christian disciple, who seeks to share his Lord in the Jesus-way (identification, demonstration, affirmation), involves himself deeply in the lives of others. He wants his Master to be seen within him. He is willing to enter into demanding relationships with others so that they can test what he has to say against the realities of their own observations. The help he has to offer is not a secondary thing which he can do long distance — stirring with a long-handled spoon. His witness is first person primary evidence.

So understanding how help happens is crucial. All too often the Christian witness has been a helper-type-let-me-change-you kind of person who is effective only at a distance of twenty-five feet or more.

But witness — done in obedient cooperation with the Holy Spirit — provides freedom to change unparalleled in human experience.

The Christian's part is simply to affirm the truth as he finds it in Jesus. Affirming is the word that puts it best for me. Most other words tend to imply pressuring, persuading, invading the other's areas of free choice.

To affirm the truth is to tell it clearly in an "affirmative" way. Not in a "directive" way as one who pretends to be an authority for the other. But affirmative, as one who stands with and not over the other.

Perhaps this can best be illustrated in parable.

If I were to tell you that the day after I complete this manuscript my family and I are driving to California, you might ask, "How will you be going?" "We'll be driving east on I-70." "East?" you might say, "Look, you poor fool, you'll never get to California going east. Shape up and get your directions straight."

To which I would reply, responding to your feelings more than your words, "If that's how you feel about me, OK. Good-bye."

You could have told me the same thing with even greater clarity, but in simple affirmation. For example, you might have said, "You're going east to California? I've found that it's 22,420 miles closer driving west." "Thank you," I'd say, "You just saved me nine months of miserable driving." "You don't know how miserable it would have been," you might say.

That too is being affirmative. It is simply to tell the truth you find in Jesus as an affirmation which respects

77

the dignity and freedom of the other person, and does it without soft-pedaling what must be said. In fact the way of affirmation is far more direct than the directive ways people often have used.

It is not being disinterested in what you are saying, it is being deeply involved in your message, and yet respecting the integrity of the hearer. Martyn Lloyd Jones writes in the devotional book *A First Book of Daily Readings:*

"I remember once reading a phrase in an article written by a man about a meeting in which he had listened to two speakers. It was a political, not a religious meeting, but what he said about those two speakers came to me as a conviction from the Holy Spirit. He said that, as he listened to the two men, he felt that this was the main difference between them: the first had spoken brilliantly as an advocate; the second as a witness. And I asked myself, which am I? Am I an advocate of these things or am I a witness? You can be an advocate of Christianity without being a Christian. You can be an advocate of these things without experiencing them. . . . You can present all the arguments. . . . And it may sound wonderful. But you may be standing outside the true experience of it the whole time. You may be talking about something which you do not really know, about someone you have never met. You are an advocate, perhaps even a brilliant advocate. But note what the Lord said to the apostles: 'Ye shall be my witnesses.' " [5]

To be a witness, boldly, radically affirmative, and at the same time gently, tenderly compassionate — this is the Jesus-way.

It must be your way — my way.

And above all, it must be authentic in unquestionably real personal experience of God. Leslie Weatherhead, the great English preacher, once said these unmistakable words on witness:

"My friends, may I warn you from my own failures that, while you will be of immense help to the cause of Christ by being able to defend its intellectual position, you will be a 10,000 times more potent missionary if you exhibit a life that Christ has changed, if you show in your nature those fruits for which all men hunger, if you have the quiet serenity, that endless good will, that deep joy, and that passionate purpose which are among the important marks of a nature surrendered to our Lord."

To give the Jesus-word in the Jesus-way, I must first affirm the worth and dignity of the other person. Then I affirm the truth as I am finding it now in Jesus. Then I affirm the options for decision that stand open before me. Many witnesses stall at this point, afraid to name the options. To voice the choice that confronts all men in accepting Christ as Savior and Lord is not an invasion of privacy.

Myron Augsburger writes helpfully at this point.

"The reluctance on the part of some people to engage in evangelism lest they violate another's freedom is a misconception of what evangelism is all about. Evangelism, when conducted in love and respect for the individual, never engages in manipulation or coercion. It is a compliment to man's freedom or ability to make a decision. When we make belief in Christ a genuine option for people we also solicit their decision. It is in the act of decision that man expresses the higher level of his moral agency. In the witness of evangelism we actually compliment man's highest level of freedom, for evangelism invites the individual to make a decision for Jesus Christ, for truth, for a new life!"[6]

Evangelism is to so present Christ that men are confronted with a true option — and a free choice to say "yes" or "no."

For Discussion
1. Have you ever — truly — been heard? Do you sometimes become very lonely for someone to listen to you?
2. Describe an experience of suffering — death of a loved one, tragedy — tell what expressions of sympathy helped. Was it a beautiful bouquet of flowery words that helped? Or simply the feeling that the other person was truly "with" you?
3. How can a person get over his selfish compulsions to be a helper-type person?
4. When people ask for help, should you give it, or will that cut you off from giving them the real help they need? Are not requests for help almost always dealing only with the symptom instead of the cause? As the crippled man at the gate "Beautiful." He asked for alms, he really needed legs. Peter refused the help he asked, and got on with the real thing.

For Assignment
1. Practice listening: 1. To a child. Sit at eye level. Play to relax the tension of the unusual, listen with your eyes, with little noises of approval, draw him out. 2. To a friend. Really try to hear what the real person is feeling. Do not interrogate, just love. 3. To someone you dislike. Try to really hear him for a change. Find something beautiful in him and express appreciation. 4. To God. Listen for one half hour of meditation a day, for one week. Keep notes on what comes up. Let your mind wander over many things, but keep it all in reference to Him.

2. Ask for the help you've been too proud to accept from a friend — a marriage partner — your pastor — a professional counselor. You must learn how it feels to be on the other end.
3. Go to someone who does not know Christ. Listen. Try to truly feel what he feels. Let him know you respect him and affirm his worth.
4. Ask a friend who may not — as far as you know — understand the gospel: "Have you ever heard anyone explain how and why she became a Christian without trying to make you do the same thing?" Then tell your story. As Nelson Kauffman advises, say, "For me, it was this way." Then in some detail (but not too detailed) tell how you received Christ, do not use the words, "you have to" do this or that. Rather say, "I felt I had to" confess, repent, etc. Allow the person to come to his own conclusion that there are things he must do to find peace . . . ask if he understood what you said . . . do not pressure anyone . . . you made your decision on your own, and he has the same right and responsibility. (Nelson Kauffman, *During the Week Witnessing,* Herald Press, p. 12.)

The
Most
Persuasive
Witness
Is living
In the presence
Of God
And loving
As He
Has commanded.

To act
In courage
When all about you
Are fearful;

To act
In hope
When your fellows
Are in despair;

To act
In love
When others
Live by hate;

To act
In forgiveness
When you are expected
To retaliate;

To live
In community
When your society
Lives in isolation;

Is witness.
Witness to the Lord
Who lives in our midst
And makes all these things possible.

WHAT THE GOSPEL IS

The Goodness of Life Together

5

The
Kingdom
Of God
"Is a community
Of right relationships."

To be
A member
Of this new
Community of Christ
Is to share
In a fellowship
Of forgiveness,
Acceptance,
And love
That draws
Others
Into
Relationship.
Into the
Common-unity
Of the life
We draw from Him.

Life together for the early Christians was good.

Jesus, their brother, had broken out of the tomb, and opened intimate communication with God for all men. The evidence that God had made this Jesus both Lord and Messiah was pulsing in their hearts and in their midst. That evidence — the Holy Spirit.

When they gathered, their fellowship was alive to the presence of Jesus. Since they knew Him to now be Lord Supreme, a political title, and Christ Messiah, the prophetic divine designation, they could ask for nothing more. They were members of His own family, blood relatives to God Himself. And more, they were now part of His body. Since His Spirit inhabited them, they were body to Him — bone, muscle, sinew, nerve cell. "In." That was the most common preposition. Christ "in" us, and we "in" Him.

There was confidence. Even exuberance. Willingness to suffer, sacrifice, share, and to be selfless.

So life together was good. They had become a community of love which was undeniably attractive to all who stepped near the circle of fellowship.

Roland Allen, one of the greatest missions authors of the last century whose books are still studied with amazement by contemporary missionaries, has this to say of New Testament church growth.

"When we turn from the restless entreaties and exhortations which fill the pages of our modern missionary magazines to the pages of the New Testament, we are astonished at the change in the atmosphere. St. Paul does not repeatedly exhort his churches to subscribe money for the propagation of the faith; he is far more concerned to explain to them what the faith is, and how they ought to practice and keep it . . . and the apostolic writers . . . do not seem to feel any necessity to repeat the Great Commission, and to urge that it is the duty of their converts to make disciples of all nations. What we read in the New Testament is not anxious appeal to Christians to spread the Gospel, but a note here and there which suggests how the Gospel was being spread abroad. . . . For centuries the Christian Church continued to expand by its own inherent grace, and threw up an increasing supply of missionaries without any direct exhortation." [1]

Something spontaneous — no — "Spiritaneous" caused growth, expansion, and eager assimilation of new people into this early fellowship of Christians. What was their secret? Perhaps a comparison — obviously exaggerated for emphasis, or is it? — will help us discover a few clues.

Early Church

And all who believed
Were together
With all in common
They sold and distributed
As any had need
And day by day,
Attending the temple together
And breaking bread
From house to house
They partook of food
With glad and generous hearts,
Praising God
And having favor with all the people.
And the Lord added to their number
Day by Day
Those who were being saved.
(Acts 2:44-47)

Our Church

Every individual,
Each with his own opinions,
Competing for his own possessions
Looks out for his own.
Assuming there are no needs
And once a week
Going to their private church
(With an annual communion)
Each return to his castle,
Fellowshiping with his family
Over good "native" cooking
After a short silent "grace,"
And glad to be away from everybody.
Occasionally there are
New faces at church.
And last year,
Someone was saved.
(Facts 19:71-72)

You fill it in

So the Word of God
Gained more and more ground.
The number of disciples . . .
Increased very greatly,
While a considerable proportion
Of even the Jewish priesthood
Accepted the faith.
 (Acts 6:7)

The whole Church . . .
Now enjoyed a period of peace.
It became established
And as it went forward
In reverence for the Lord
And in the strengthening presence of the Holy Spirit
Continued to grow in numbers.°
 (Acts 9:31)

Consequently the Churches
Grew stronger and stronger
In the faith
And their numbers
Increased daily.²
 (Acts 16:5)

"SPIRITANEOUS" GROWTH

There is something so unselfconscious, so seemingly natural and spontaneous in these "field notes" from the early church, coupled as they are to the Christ-centered teaching of the new life, and devoid as they indeed are from all the commands to evangelize. (One exception, "Do the work of an evangelist," the 2 Timothy 4:5 warning against being a timid Tim.) The emphasis in the New Testament seemed to be on the quality of the Christian life, its potential, its possibilities, and above all on the power — the Holy Spirit — and the Lord — the God-man Jesus. But there is a great silence on the need, importance, and incentives to witness. The work of evangelism seems to be assumed as the inevitable and unavoidable by-product or result of living the new life. What connection can there be between the emphasis and the silence? Does it imply that when the interior life of a Christian fellowship truly represents and honors her Lord, then evangelism will follow as a necessary outcome?

It is clear that Jesus expected every disciple to be a witness by virtue of his own experience of the Holy Spirit's presence. But it is equally clear that He expected this witness to be a corporate — community — group — fellowship — church — embodied witness. His commissions were given in plural word forms. "We" are to witness. Not as loners, but as brothers. It is for "us" to share the good news of God's love in Jesus, not as individuals, but as persons in relationship to both God and man.

The idea of the "individual" (each man is an island, unique, alone, sufficient in himself) is a nonbiblical concept. Even unbiblical. Both Old and New Testament view us not as individuals, but as "persons" — persons who live in right relationships to both God and man. Individuals may associate;

persons relate. Individuals may even communicate; persons commune.

In the New Testament it is assumed that no disciple of Christ can make an adequate profession of his faith apart from membership in the Christian community. The early church brothers "devoted themselves to fellowship." To speak of solitary Christians is biblical nonsense. The word "saint" does not occur, but "saints" is often used.

It is said one Englishman is a gentleman, two a tea party, three and you have the British Empire. So one Christian — is a prayer, two a church, three a denomination. In the words of Jesus, one, two, three, He is in the midst and church is happening.

To know Christ is to live in relationship. It is to participate in "the Kingdom of right relationships which," says Bruce Larson, "is one description of the Kingdom of God."[3]

RELATIONAL WITNESS

Richard Halverson, in his position paper on personal evangelism given to the Berlin Congress of 1966, stressed the power of relationships in the Christian community. It must be quoted in length.

"In the apostolic Church, the relation between believers and God and among fellow believers was paramount. The light and warmth and love, the forgiveness and acceptance that emanated from that unique community penetrated a jaded, bored, loveless, weary culture and awakened the spiritual hunger of both Jew and pagan. 'Lo, how they love one another!' it was said of them; sin-sick, fed-up men tried to understand the strange and inviting quality of life that marked the disciples.

"Today in personal evangelism the tendency is to ignore the relations within the Christian community and to be preoccupied with the individual Christian's relation to those outside the Church. As a consequence, one of the greatest stumbling blocks to the world outside the Church is the way Christians treat one another. Today's world might be inclined to say with some justification as it views the Church, 'Lo, how they dislike one another!' The faithful work of zealous Christians in personal evangelism is often neutralized by the attitudes and actions within the Christian family. The corporate image of the Church often nullifies the faithful witness of individual members. And there is that peculiar phenomenon, the zealous Christian who in his desire to do personal work walks a guarded, careful way among unbelievers but who within the Christian community acts like the devil himself.

"Jesus said, 'By this shall all men know that ye are my disciples, if ye have love one to another' (John 13:35).

"All evangelism is born out of such a relationship, and personal evangelism in the true New Testament sense will be the inevitable and abundant fruit of such renewal in the Church. Outside this context, methods of personal evangelism can be perilous indeed. Methods wrongly born may attract, indoctrinate, and regiment certain zealous persons in a way that produces self-conscious, 'spiritually elite' individuals preoccupied with 'results,' who tend to think of themselves as superior to those not so inclined. This kind of situation militates against the fellowship and hence defeats witness. We do not discredit methods properly taught and practiced (the Holy Spirit uses means); we insist, rather, that they always be kept in the context of the total life of the Christian community and subordinate to the ministry of the Spirit of God within believers as individuals and as a body."[4]

RENEWAL OR EXPANSION?

"Before we can witness, we must have renewal, revival, perhaps even resurrection," say many.

Tom Allan, in his book *The Face of My Parish*, says, "It is a mistake to say we must cleanse the inner life of our church before we undertake the work of evangelism, and strengthen the faithful before we set about reclaiming the lapsed or challenging the careless. The faithful can only be strengthened in so far as they are going out to the lapsed and the careless. The inner life of the church can only gain reality in so far as the church is meeting its missionary responsibilities."[5]

Allan is right, renewal cannot happen until there is renewed faithfulness in open relationships outside the church as well as inside. Believers can be renewed only as we reach out to share Christ's life-changing love.

Donald McGavran, missionary, church-growth leader, teacher of missions, writes incisively: "Is renewal the first need of the church, or expansion? The great need of the world and the great commission of our Lord is simultaneous advance both to make disciples and to perfect. It is not either/or. It is both/and.

"Real renewal issues in a passion to bring others (now outside the Church) into redemptive relationship with Christ. Multitudes of new Christians feeding on the Word, lifted by the fellowship of the Church, and available to the Holy Spirit are the surest way to renewal.

"How do we know that the purposes of God must *first* be filled by renewing us, the 'old Christian'? That is not the New Testament way. Had God the Holy Spirit waited till the Jewish Christian community at Jerusalem all by itself broke the barrier to the Gentiles, He would have waited a long time. Instead, the fresh advance of the Christian faith, the new relevancy to the Gentile world was achieved by baptizing hordes of those who in the year 50 A.D. were outside the Church.

"Let us then be done with petty criticism of evangelism and church growth. Let us be done with depreciation of renewal. We must have such renewal that multitudes will be willing to die that others know Christ. We must have such church growth that the divine life becomes available to hundreds of millions now out of the Church and thus leads them both to live holy lives and to create a holy society."[6]

THE FELLOWSHIP OF THE SPIRIT

Simultaneous breakthrough in both renewal and reaching out can be nothing less than a breaking out of the Holy Spirit from the rigid confinements we constantly encrust about Him. The spontaneous growth of the early Christian fellowships is credited solely to the Holy Spirit. There can be no avoiding this conclusion as you survey the Acts and the epistles, with a view on the contrasts between the working of the Spirit and the demonic. These contrasts are most helpful when the context of each is examined carefully. They are things which happen not primarily to the individual, but to the Koinonia groups of the body of Christ.

The Spirit of Christ	*The Demonic*
He gives life (Jn. 6:63)	It deals in death (Heb. 2:14, 15)
He sets us free (2 Cor. 3:17)	It binds men (Lk. 13:16; Acts 10:38)
He reveals truth (Jn. 14:16; 15:26)	It multiplies lies (Jn. 8:44; Acts 5:3)

He is our memory bank (Jn. 14:26)	It nags us doggedly (1 Tim. 2:6, 7; 1 Pet. 5:8)
He is our advocate with God (Rom. 8:26)	It accuses and condemns (Rev. 12:10)
He communicates the Word (1 Thess. 1:5)	It snatches the Word away (Mk. 4:15)
He commissions men to witness (Acts 13:2)	It sifts them like chaff. (Lk. 22:31)
He releases men to speak (Mt. 10:19, 20; Acts 2:4)	It hinders the witness (1 Thess. 2:18; Jude 9)
He provides new light and insight (Jn. 16:8)	It blinds the mind and will (2 Cor. 4:4)
He liberates from the power of sin (Rom. 8:2)	It ensnares and enslaves (2 Tim. 2:26)

(The demonic powers deserve only the neuter pronoun, "it," not because they are nonpersonal, but because they are anti-personal, destroying all true personhood.)

But He — the abiding presence of the Lord Jesus known as the Holy Spirit of God — when given full right to reign can give life, freedom, vitality, power to communicate, vision for witness, liberty to speak — all the gifts needed in a fellowship of Christians.

In any given group of persons open to the Spirit, all necessary gifts can be present. He releases them to form a body, with nothing lacking. He provides all the peculiar gifts needed to complete the fellowship in its full work of being and giving the good news. The only necessary steps on your part are: (1) faith to believe that every needed gift is present in your midst, (2) love, to encourage brothers/sisters to discover every gift that is present within them, and (3) humility to recognize a greater gift in another, and encourage it, when God has called you to a smaller one.

When Christians are alive to the Holy Spirit's presence in their midst, they come alive to each other in a new way. A different atmosphere pervades the group.

Mutual concern radiates to meet each other's needs. (Examine Philippians 2:1-4.)

Shared encouragement listens to hear and understand the other's defeats and supplies strength where it is needed. (Examine 1 Peter 3:8-15.)

Continuing forgiveness is extended freely to others, just as it has been received from the Lord Jesus. (Examine Colossians 3:12-17.)

A vulnerable honesty trusts others with failures and defeats as well as with dreams and high intentions. (Examine 1 John 1:5-10.)

Compassion, the compelling love of Jesus, reaches out to draw others into the circle of faith. (Examine 2 Corinthians 5:5-21.)

Such an atmosphere of the Spirit is alive with contagion. It communicates itself both verbally and nonverbally. And irresistibly!

NO OTHER OPTIONS

To be a fellowship of the Spirit inevitably results in becoming a fellowship in witness. If either one is absent, the other cannot be marked present. Where He is present in His power, men are witnesses. It was as simple, as clear, as final as that in Christ's words, and it has been proven equally true in life (Acts 1:8, Church History AD 30 — 1973).

There is nothing optional about witness to the Christ. If you know Him, you affirm Him to others by word and deed. If you love Him, you live His love to those about you. If you follow Him in life, you are being a witness daily. (But you cannot assume that all of life is mission, so you need put no effort, no priority on communicating the good news. When all is mission soon nothing is mission.)

Nor do you presume that witness — being spontaneous — needs no effort nor emphasis in your schedule. To say I never need to plan any word or deed to share my Christ, I just let my life naturally show it, is unbearable self-righteousness. No one has a life that is good enough to tell of Jesus without affirmations of who-what-why.

There are no options — for those who choose to follow Jesus daily — than to consider the communication of God's good word in Jesus as the central fact of life. To follow Jesus is to so order priorities, vocation, values, relationships, group loyalties, possessions, service, and affirmations so that others will know unmistakably that you are Christ's. And that He is your Lord.

When groups of Christians experience the quality of life together that is available to them in Jesus, it is good. So good that it shows on them. The word gets around. It's attractive. Others want to be a part of it too. The witness wins them.

It's the goodness of life together.

For Discussion

1. Which must come first — renewal or expansion? Can renewal come unless we are faithful in reaching outward? Does renewal usually come through the experience of seeing persons coming to new life in Christ? Why?
2. If the Holy Spirit were suddenly taken from your congre-

gation, what things would be able to go on with no noticeable change? What would change? Do you need any of those things that would go on unaffected?
3. If you were more concerned about the relational dimensions of Christian living than the factual, the doctrinal, the philosophical, and the theological, would it not eliminate a lot of talk, a lot of routine ritual, and free you to get at the good parts of life together?
4. Is not revival simply — beginning to live relationally — open to God (no roof), open to each other (no walls), and open about ourselves (no closets)?

For Assignment

1. Compile as complete a list as possible of your congregation's alumni association. People still living in driving distance, but no longer associated with you. (Dropouts before baptism age, married outs, walked outs, drifted outs, shutouts, churched outs, transferred outs.) Write down why you think they stepped outside your relationships and fellowship. Now go listen to them — undefensively. Find out why they can live better without your group of Christians, or what they are finding elsewhere that is more important.
2. Ask others how they are experiencing the presence of the Holy Spirit. Talk to someone who is deeply aware of His presence through simple obedience to the Word. Listen to someone from the charismatic movement. Ask yourself, "What is authentic? Where is the love?" Listen for His leading.
3. Ask your youth for a good reading on the quality of fellowship and the relationships being experienced in your church. Don't discuss it with others, just choose one weak point and resolve to do your part in seeing it change.

4. Begin a prayer cell group, without letting anyone know whose idea it was or how it got started.

No
Longer
Orphaned,
We are God's sons.

No Longer
Aliens,
We are at home with heaven.

No Longer
Enemies,
We are the friends of God.

No
Longer
Strangers,
We can know and be known.

So
We
Live it in return;
Adopting orphans,
Assimilating aliens,
Befriending enemies,
Absorbing strangers.

It is the way of Jesus.
It was His way with us.
It is His way for us.

HOW TO COMMUNICATE IT

Following Jesus Daily in Life   6

***The
Only
Organization
In
The
World
Which
Does
Not
Exist
For
Its
Own
Sake
Or for
The sake
Of its
Members
Is the
Church of Jesus Christ!***

"No man can know Christ truly
Except he follow Him daily in life."

So wrote early Anabaptist evangelist Hans Denk, expressing the conviction that not only salvation but also ethics and moral decisions are intimately related to the cross of Jesus.

To know Christ is to follow Him.

To follow Him is to give second place to vocation, work, and things (boat, nets, the net price of salt fish) and to place persons and the person of Jesus first. (I will make you to become a netsman of men.)

To follow Him is to become a part of an interwoven community — "The kingdom of heaven is like unto a great drawnet — which cast into the world draws men to the Savior and Lord of all" (Mt. 13:47-50).

Brothers and sisters of Jesus, intertwined in fellowship and mutual commitment, can sweep through a community gently drawing men and women together and bringing them near to their Lord.

Such a community is inner-controlled (by Christ) and outer directed (by that same Lord). It is an open-ended fellowship. Like a drawnet, it is impossible to avoid. Too many churches are like hook and line. Little hook, much sinker, no food to invite the hungry, and all too easily avoidable.

It was said of the early church that it was easy to join, but hard to stay in; while fellowships today are hard to join (closed door policies) and impossible to get out. Often churches have assumed that the only way to keep the demands of discipleship high is to man the doors with inspectors and guards. That assumption seems to be "screen them at the gate, keep out undesirables, and you will preserve the integrity of your memberships." It obviously does not work on more than a superficial level. Integrity of discipleship occurs only when there is a covenant reaffirmed voluntarily by participating persons at important points in their maturing pilgrimage together, a covenant to follow Jesus daily, and to make His book their handbook for life. If the demands are high, cannot the gate be left unguarded?

THE CHURCH — NOT FOR SINNERS?

"The church is not for sinners," one counselor who works with troubled people concludes. "The church has become the place where people can come together once a week to reaffirm a sense of well-being and acceptance in society. They come not out of a sense of guilt or sinfulness, but to make overt manifestation of their righteousness and goodness. Most churchgoers look on the fallen with scorn and distrust; they would find it practically impossible to speak to the needs of a recognized sinner." [1]

Those words come from the bitter disappointment of one who has given his life to assist ex-convicts rehabilitate themselves, only to find the church a community of rejection, not acceptance.

"I worked for five years to inspire lay-witness," a pastor told me. "During the last year, there were four witness-oriented prayer cells making contacts with troubled persons, and leading them to faith in Christ. Eight couples committed themselves that year. I attempted to fellowship, counsel, and support them. Then when illness took me away, they one by one slipped out of the circle. The alcoholics, back to their drinking, the others drifted into circles of pleasure-oriented people who gave them acceptance. No one seemed to sense that they were starving for fellowship. Everyone went about business as usual and let their interest and new faith die.

"We needed not just to inspire core goups to begin reaching out, but to turn our whole membership face-outward, in an every-member-mobilization. Not to a program, but to person-centered living, fellowship, and time schedules. Our church was structured for the total good of the in-group, or in-families, better said, and not for the good of those who were invited to become fellow travelers."

STRUCTURE FOR EXTENSION OR PRESERVATION?

"A congregation should be oriented toward those outside itself," writes Myron Augsburger, "it should be structured for extension more than preservation.

"Too much of our energy as a church goes into defensive measures. Consequently we often develop a religious inferiority-complex. . . . The degree in which we mobilize a congregation to be effective exponents of Christian faith will determine our success in attracting others to the faith. This means developing an evangelistic atmosphere and approach to community involvement. Small groups of various types can serve as nuclei of reconciling love. The Christian family continues to be one of the most powerful instruments of witness." [2]

Cells of persons who "get together, get started, and get going," as Sam Shoemaker used to put it, can gather for prayer and Spirit-controlled consensus, and go out to find where Christ is at work in His world and become co-workers. (Not to take Christ there, but to go where He is, and share in His work.)

Encounter groups, for persons who need to find release spiritually, emotionally, and empathetically, can provide a context of freedom in which Christians can grow in self-understanding, and in being understanding of others. Through personal relationships members can learn love, forgiveness, and acceptance. Such a group should rapidly mature into a witness group whose gathering is seen as a report-repower session in preparation for scattering into their work-block-recreation-friendship circles for new witness. If its focus does not turn outward after a minimum of six months . . . there is serious need for rethinking its purpose.

Nurture groups may be formed to provide acceptance, sharing, and intimate support to new Christians. Or this function may be a part of the agenda of groups previously described. Or in a small congregation, the whole group may share in all functions. The important thing is finding your own fellowship's unique way of directing its energies outward to become a Christian presence, a Christian power, a Christ-proclamation.

BECOMING A CHRISTIAN PRESENCE

When the good news creates a people who are themselves a word of good news to the community, their "presence" produces an alteration of the atmosphere which allows the

Spirit of God to work more freely in persons, and in the structures made by people.

There is a "Christian presence" in the community when those who follow Jesus accept the task of becoming "standard setters." Not in coercive fashion, but in visible demonstration of life governed by the Jesus-ethic. Infiltration of the educational system, both as teachers and as parents, can influence standards. The same is true for recreational commissions, business organizations, chambers of commerce, race relations councils, housing commissions, open housing action groups, the list can be lengthened in every community.

If you view the broad profile of citizens around you, they tend to grade themselves out into various functions. (This is true today as in the Book of Acts.)

There are the "censors" — the critics who are slow to accept change. They may be public appointees — judges, commissioners, bishops, etc., or self-appointed censors. They are hard to reach, hard to influence, almost impossible to change. Still, Paul tried; he spoke to the Pharisees, he appealed to Nero.

There are the "creators" — the idea people, the educational eggheads, the opinion formers, the pacesetters of the community. They are innovators who like new things, the crusaders who pursue causes. Here Paul did well, he addressed Festus, Felix, Agrippa, Sergius Paulus, the Mars' Hill audience.

There are the "receivers" — the great majority of people who do their work, and do not ask many of the larger questions of who they are or where they came from. "The fat bulk," some call them. "The silent majority," perhaps. Paul didn't neglect these in his general preaching and work. He worked with them continually.

Finally, there are the "activists" — the people who are out and around doing; the people who are mobilizing people for action. They get the real work done on the projects the "creators" may spawn. They may be doctors or barbers, union leaders or social workers, pastors, or teachers. They are found in every profession or skill. (If they're getting something accomplished.) This is the point of Paul's greatest fruitfulness, in marketplace, synagogue, and school.

Christian "presence" participates with all these people in their various functions seeking to leaven their insights with the truth of the gospel, to call them to higher concerns for the good of all, and to attract them to the consideration of Jesus, confronting them with the need for personal decision-making.

As "standard setters," Christians also function as discussion starters. Being present where the real hurts of the world are felt, they can hear the real questions that are asked. The world asks its questions about man/life/meaning/goals, and Christians, made sensitive by the Spirit, must be there to hear them, and to affirm the answers He finds.

The world's questions are often the wrong questions. Man's questions tend to be non-questions, circular questions that leap from symptom to symptom and never get to the cause. The Spirit-sensitized person can gently suggest what the real question is, and let that planted seed slowly mature.

And there are moments when the Christian must ask the real questions — ask them loudly (shout them from the housetop) so that the truth is unavoidable and must be faced.

"Discussion starters" can then move on to witness to their confidence in Jesus. They can serve as inspirers, confidence-builders, and motivators.

And Christians, truly present where the hurts of their

communities lie open, must be reconcilers, peacemakers, and bridge builders between those now estranged. As reconcilers, they may even need to absorb much of that hurt and suffering upon themselves, acting to buffer the hyperacidity of those who cannot stomach each other. (A parable: acid and alkali combined produce salt. When the gentle alkaline solution of love absorbs the acids of hate, have I not become the salt of the earth?)

A Christian presence, energized by the Holy Spirit, is a Christian power. Not power over others — that is coercive power, dominating power. It is power to become adequate for life's difficult situation. Power to love where hate seems the only normal response. Power to forgive when resentment and retaliation seem the responsible thing. Power to endure when the suffering seems beyond the threshold of patience.

A Christian presence is power to dream dreams of new things the Spirit of God can do in and through fellowship in the community. It is power to bring dreams to reality. All this is the birthright of those who are born anew of the Holy Spirit.

Such "overstatements," as people tend to classify them, are far from the normal stuff of life, so man seldom dreams, and seldom reaches out to fulfill the ordinary day-to-day visions, of letting his life be all that it can become.

HE CAN COMMUNICATE THROUGH US

If I am willing to be present with the Holy Spirit in the common affairs of men, to be obedient to Him in service to the common needs of men, He releases an uncommon power within me. It is a power to communicate.

It can and does happen in the most commonplace situations, through the most unremarkable persons. The Spirit's ability to break through is not limited by the talents of the witness, but by the faithfulness shown in simple response to His Spirit.

Recognizing that He asks us to simply be present — truly present by giving a gift of loving presence to others — any of us, indeed all of us, can begin to be faithful. And understanding that witness is simply a matter of affirming what Jesus Christ is doing in my life, I have no excuse not to share, neither does anyone else.

It is not the unusual or the bizarre that is needed, it is doing the simple obvious thing that is so necessary.

It is not a big-business organization that your congregations need, but faithful people who will covenant to begin doing what they've known they could do all along. Love people. And drop His name into the conversation. Credit Him as the source of it all.

It is not clever strategy and brilliant administration (along with good sharp mimeographing) that will bring in the kingdom. It is simply living "the kingdom of right relationships" now. And letting the "why" come through in attitudes and words.

COVENANT COMMUNITIES UNDER CHRIST

Christian congregations, to share faithfully in their Lord's work in His world, must covenant together before God and each other (is not this the meaning of baptism?) to carry out the commission as it applies in their situations.

Their covenant should be specific, and stated in clear measurable terms.

To: be a community of the love of God which is clearly visible and recognizable by others as an evidence of His presence among men. (Thus anything which would mar that witness must be confessed openly, forgiven readily, and the freshness so experienced used as a base for further witness to Christ's redeeming work.

To: be a body of ministering disciples, not inner directed in self-serving ministries, but pointed out in service beyond the congregation to enrich and liberate the lives of neighbors, friends, and enemies. So each person is assisted in defining the ministry open to him, and in exercising it as a specific service to human need — physical and/or spiritual. (The internal functions are important and are to be shared out among members. But they are no exemption from carrying a primary commission for work "out there.")

To: creatively explore, discover, and release every gift in every member. Where a gift seems to be lacking or only partially developed, others encourage that person to become all he or she can be in Christ, and assist in facilitating that release. It is a prerequisite for the release of His gifts in full power that every member pray earnestly for every other that all the potential God has invested within him/her may be exercised to its greatest capacity.

To: constantly look for the new fronts for witness, to discover where the responses are to evangelism and concentrate the efforts there; to note where the needs are felt and open to loving service — be it drug addiction, alcoholism, unwed mothers, draftees searching for alternatives, families in conflict, marriages nearing estrangement, emotional health approaching fatigue and breakdown, or depression.

To: dream dreams and set guidelines for long-term witness. For example, recognize that congregational growth of less than 2.5 percent is failing to break even, to assume that growth should normally be 15 percent per annum, 2.5 percent by simple biology, growing, and attracting your own to Christ, 2.5 percent by transfer from people constantly moving into our communities, and 10 percent by conversion. This is neither a dream nor a goal, it is simply a normal scale for natural growth. To dream is to reach out beyond such assumptions.

To: be constantly aware of the urgency of the task — to share the good news — and of the eternal significance of the invitation Christ extends through them. There is only one forgiveness, one redeeming sacrifice of life, blood, of God Himself; one way to be reconciled for ever; it is through Jesus Christ alone.

To: be awake to the impending appearance of the Lord Christ. In a constant atmosphere of expectancy, the covenant community accepts the tasks of witness and service, knowing that at any moment they may be interrupted by the appearance of Jesus in visible form. He is coming. Soon.

But until then, we who are members of His intimate fellowship-body here must discern, decide, dream, and do.

We can affirm:

Jesus is all.

Jesus is all powerful.

Jesus is all powerful in us.

Jesus is all powerful in us now.

For Discussion

1. When Christ is in your midst as you gather in groups, can an unsaved person come into that group without confronting Christ and feeling His magnetic pull?
2. In fellowship evangelism, can your groups deliberately covenant to surround unsaved persons with the loving warmth and power of Christian fellowship and lead them to meet the Lord Jesus?
3. The fellowship of Christians is not only a result of the gospel, it is part of the gospel itself. Is it, therefore, a basic contradiction in the idea that the gospel could be faithfully proclaimed by one person?
4. What dreams should you be dreaming for more effective presence, for more released exercise of Christian power, for more clear and faithful witness?

For Assignment

1. Draw up a covenant which you feel a faithful Christian group should be willing to pledge. Then rewrite it into the kind of covenant you could conscientiously commit yourself to carry out.
2. Dream goals for your fellowship on a graduated five-year-plan — growth — new projects — stewardship — daughter cells forming new congregations — bring your dream to share with the others.
3. Plan a pastor-layman teamwork approach for on-the-job training in personal witness. Since sharing faith is actually learned not in a classroom, but in the living room, lunchroom, or recreation room, and ways of sharing Christ are better shown than told, more caught than taught, therefore — come up with the concrete suggestions for your congregation.
4. Volunteer to go with your pastor for an evening of home visits. Ask him about exploring a two or three to a team plan for making contacts in the homes of your community.
5. Begin to think broadly of ways to minister cooperatively with other Christian groups to infiltrate, influence, and/or have prophetic impact on every strata and subgroup in your community. Not just a cooperative crusade, but interdenominational prayer groups, study groups, action groups, ministry planning task forces, special interest missions. Vision!

FOOTNOTES

Chapter One

1. Report from Yaounde Consultation, quoted in *Church Growth Bulletin*, March 1966, Vol. II, No. 4, p. 3
2. Lesslie Newbigin, *International Review of Missions*, Editorial, April 1965.
3. David A Shank, *Who Will Answer?* Herald Press, Scottdale, Pa., 1969, pp. 28-32.

Chapter Two

1. Albert van den Heuvel, unpublished address given at St. Petersburg, Fla., December 8, 1970.
2. Bernie Wiebe, *Sharing My Christian Faith*, Mennonite Radio Mission publication, Winnipeg, Manitoba, June 1966.
3. Paul Tournier, *The Meaning of Persons*, Harper and Row, New York, 1957, p. 22.

Chapter Three

1. Elton Trueblood, *The New Man for Our Time*, Harper and Row, New York, 1970, p. 25.
2. Ibid., p. 32.
3. William Stringfellow, *My People Is the Enemy*, Holt, Rinehart, and Winston, Inc. New York, 1964, p. 32.
4. Peter J. Dyck, "When Is Service Christian?" MCC News Service, May 24, 1968.
5. From *The New Testament in Modern English*, © J. B. Phillips, 1958. Used by permission of the Macmillan Company.
6. Phillips, Ibid.
7. Lesslie Newbigin, *One Body, One Gospel, One World*, Harper Brothers, New York, p. 22.
8. Dyck, op. cit., pp. 7, 8.
9. Everett C. Parker, "Christian Communication and Secular Man," an unpublished manuscript released by the Office of Communication, United Church of Christ, New York.
10. As quoted by Samuel H. Moffett, "What Is Evangelism?" *Christianity Today*, August 22, 1969, p. (1013) 5.

Chapter Four

1. Phillips, op. cit.
2. David A. Redding, "The Last Altar Call," *Christianity Today*, Washington, Dec. 22, 1967, p. (277) 5.
3. Dr. Allan Keith-Lucas, "Helping People Is a Ticklish Business," a paper given to representatives of the helping professions, Mental Health Associations of South Carolina. Reprinted in the *Christian Scholar*.
4. *Ibid.*
5. Martyn Lloyd Jones, *A First Book of Daily Readings*, Eerdmans, as quoted in *Pulpit Digest*, February 1971, p. 26.
6. Myron Augsburger, "Evangelism for the 70's," 1970 CMPA Lecture, *The Canadian Mennonite*, Winnipeg, May 15, 1970, p. 7.

Chapter Five

1. Roland Allen, *The Spontaneous Expansion of the Church*, Grand Rapids, Michigan: William B. Eerdmans, 1962, p. 6.
2. Phillips, op. cit.
3. Bruce Larson, *No Longer Strangers*, Word, Waco, Texas, 1971.
4. Richard C. Halverson, "Methods of Personal Evangelism." *Christianity Today*, October 28, 1966, p. 27 [91].
5. Tom Allan, *The Face of My Parish*, p. 50.
6. Donald McGavran, Church Growth Bulletin (Pasadena: Fuller Theological Seminary, January 1966), pp. 7, 8.

Chapter Six

1. Lucius B. Lyman, Jr., "The Church Is Not for Sinners," *The Christian Century*, July 17, 1968, p. 919.
2. Myron Augsburger, "Evangelism for the 70's," CMPA Lecture for 1970, *Canadian Mennonite*, May 15, 1970, p. 6.

Photo Credits: Cover and pages 47 and 63, Wallowitch; pages 7 and 29, Rohn Engh; page 83, Phil Knepper; page 99, Paul M. Schrock.